Praise for

THE UNEMPLOYMENT SURVIVAL HANDBOOK
by Nina Schuyler

"Remember the good old days, when authors wrote about career success and employment opportunities? Well, prepare yourself for the mid-1990s, when books like *THE UNEMPLOYMENT SURVIVAL HANDBOOK* replace those more positive topics. In this survival manual, legal journalist Nina Schuyler covers every aspect of this unfortunately increasingly common situation, from filing for unemployment benefits to stress management. Not surprisingly, considering her background, the focus is on the legal ramifications. Schuyler uses case studies throughout the handbook, which help to illustrate her recommendations."

—Small Press

"...Schuyler uses common scenarios to illustrate the basics of the unemployment safety net and hence assuages the immediate worry of the newly laid off: how to qualify for benefits. As employers have a built-in incentive to contest claims (for they must pay into the fund for each valid claim), she explains their potential wiles, as well as the rules, slightly different among the 50 states, by which bureaucrats calculate eligibility. If they pronounce the dreaded word "Benefits denied," quasi-legal appeals are possible but require careful preparation and civil argumentation. She lists sources of help for that...and concludes her functional tract with a chapter of generic job-hunting tips."

—Booklist

"Most job-hunting books describe unemployment as a condition that can be overcome relatively quickly. This book is for the many who find unemployment to be a long and stressful period. Schuyler, a legal journalist, combines a thorough description of eligibility and filing requirements with common-sense advice on how unemployment recipients can get the money they are entitled to without sacrificing their dignity....Recommended."

—Library Journal

THE UNEMPLOYMENT SURVIVAL HANDBOOK

THE UNEMPLOYMENT SURVIVAL HANDBOOK

by

Nina Schuyler

ALLWORTH PRESS, NEW YORK

Published by Allworth Press, an imprint of Allworth Communications, Inc., 10 East 23rd Street, New York, NY 10010.

Distributor to the trade in the United States:
Consortium Book Sales & Distribution, Inc.,
1045 Westgate Drive, Saint Paul, MN 55114–1065.

Book design by Douglas Design Associates, New York, NY.

ISBN: 1-880559-08-0

Library of Congress Catalog Card Number: 92-75525

Table of Contents

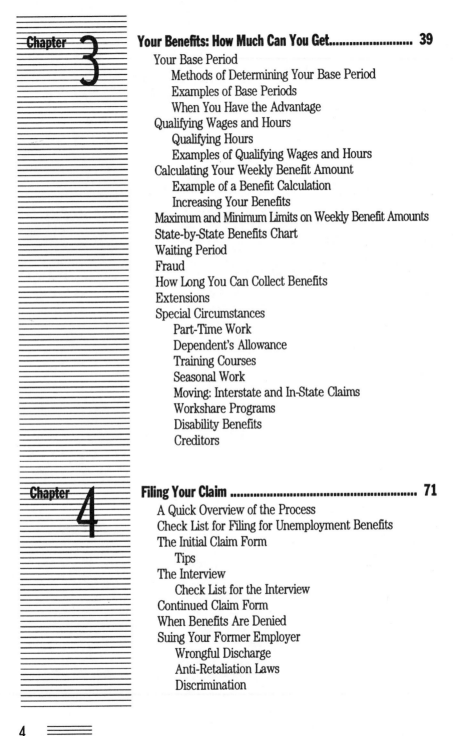

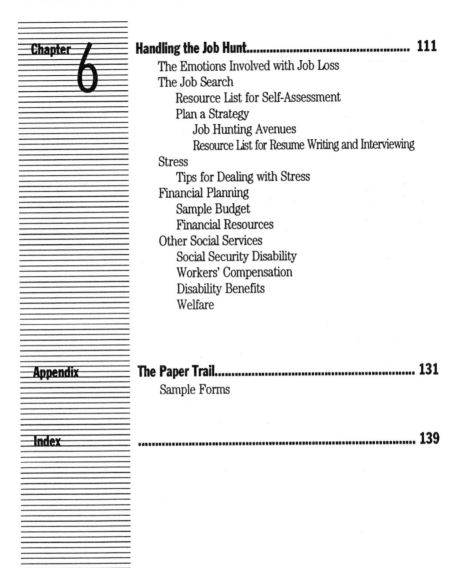

Chapter 1

In Between Jobs

t's Monday morning. The bus rattles by and you hear the familiar sound of your neighbor reving the car's engine. Someone calls out to hurry because the bus is here. Children's voices float below your window as they head to school. Sunshine peeks into your room from the bathroom window and a patch of it settles on your face, still nestled in a pillow. The air feels crisp. You're about to throw off the bed covers and join the Monday morning sprint to work. But then you remember: you lost your job last week. Your stomach turns into twisted pretzel and you pull the sheets closer.

Chances that you will lose your job at least once during your working life are greater than they've ever been before. Almost everyday, there's an article about more lay offs: IBM cuts 40,000, General Motors lays off 74,000 and Pacific Bell chops 11,000 employees. It's number like these that mean you will be looking for a job six to eight times during your lifetime. Although it's unlikely you'll hear, "You're fired," you are likely to be told that you are being terminated, dehired, severed, or voluntarily separated. Or that you are included in a downsizing plan, a retrenchment, restructuring, or merger. Whatever your former employer chose to call it, one thing has remained the same: the gut-wrenching reaction you have when you lose your job. Almost everyone experiences shock, anger, and surprise, plus a psychological inability to deal with these emotions. You suffer from lack of confidence at the very time that you must face a host of practical problems like scrambling for a scarce job and grappling with rising personal debts.

It is through work that we express ourselves. How often have you been asked at a party, "What do you do?" And how difficult is it then to say you are unemployed? Instead, you skirt the question, answering, "I am in between things." It is through work that we can challenge ourselves and learn. And it is through work that we meet people and form friendships. In our society, identity is derived from our occupations. It is often who we become and who we are. When we lose our jobs, we often lose our sense of self and control over our lives. "When you're out of work for a while, you begin to wonder whether you're worth anything," said Don Heisler, 54, an unemployed engineer. Our anxiety only increases as we watch our bank account start to plummet. What will happen to the car, house, the family bills? How will we pay for the mortgage or rent, the doctor's bills and food? We feel like it's the end of the world.

But it's not.

Overview of the Book

Unlike most books that skim right over this anxiety-ridden period, this one gives you practical advice on how to handle both the emotional and financial issues that you now face. This book supplies the tools to deal with this difficult time and to help you understand that it's not the end of the world. Through this understanding, you will gain more control of your life. Although there are no short cuts to escape your anger and frustration over your job loss, you can learn to act rather than react. Part of acting is starting your search for a new job. Here, you will find a brief summary of different ways to locate a job. A recent study showed that the more avenues you use to find one, the greater your job hunting success. Here you have a road map of the most commonly used ways to find a job. You will discover those avenues that work better than others. A list of books to help you assess your skills and prepare your resume and for your job interview is provided at the end of this chapter.

But the bulk of this book speaks to the heart of your anxiety—money. Most of *The Unemployment Survival Handbook* addresses your need for money. Not just any money, but money that you are entitled to receive—your unemployment benefits. As you clocked in the hours for your last employers, they were paying a certain tax, which went into a special fund. That money is designated by the state for times like this, when you are out of a job. This is not welfare. Instead, it is very similar to receiving social security payments upon retirement: you are entitled to unemployment benefits, whether you are rich or poor, if you are out of work through no fault of your own. This book will walk you through the unemployment insurance benefits system step-by-step to show you how to receive the money that is rightfully yours.

The sole purpose of this money is to help you through the transition to a new job. We no longer function in an era where we work thirty years for one employer and are handed generous promotions, benefits, pay increases, and job security. Now lay offs affect nearly everyone at one point during their career. Virtually every industry in America—from banking, finance, advertising, and retail to construction and agriculture—is experiencing massive changes. By now, everyone talks casually about mergers, reorganizations, downsizing, and buy-outs, and most have been affected by these management tools. This kind of management has become part of our culture. Now, you will be retraining and retooling, working for several different employers in your lifetime. More than at any other time in history, people are experiencing time out of work because of job changes.

Chapter two, on eligibility, carefully explains what criteria you must meet to receive unemployment insurance benefits. Real cases decided by different states' appeals boards are used to illustrate the common ways you can lose your job and still receive benefits. The fundamental question asked in each of these examples is: "Whose fault is it that you are now out of a job?" If you can honestly say that it isn't your fault, you're on your way to receiving unemployment benefits. But even if it isn't your fault, you will find out in this chapter why you should expect your former employer to argue otherwise. Your employer may claim that you were let go because of misconduct. You will come to understand what is meant by that term and how to determine if your behavior rose to that level of fault. You will learn that in many cases, what your former employer calls misconduct is really poor performance or carelessness, which still allows you to collect benefits.

You also must show that you are able and available for work for each week that you wish to receive benefits. If you decide to completely change your career from construction to teaching, but you lack the skills to teach, you will be considered unavailable for work and won't receive benefits. You've taken yourself out of the job market, because you need to go back to school and get the necessary training to teach. On the other hand, if you have some teaching experience and can show that you meet the job market criteria for teachers, you will most likely receive your benefits.

The final criterion introduced in this chapter is something called a "suitable job offer." You have started your job hunt and, several weeks later, you receive a job offer for a position that you don't really want. You will learn when you can reject that offer and still receive benefits.

Chapter three, on benefits, introduces several more qualifications that you must meet to receive benefits. Almost all states require you to have earned a minimum amount of wages during a certain period of time. Some states also require you to have worked a minimum amount of hours. These requirements are called your "qualifying wage and hours." Extensive charts are included, which indicate the qualifying wage and hours for your state.

You are also given your state's formula for calculating your weekly benefit amount. Each state uses a slightly different calculation to determine your weekly benefit check. This chapter is the most technical because of this calculation. It also involves the most specialized language— base period, base year, waiting period. Each of these terms is explained in great detail, so that you will understand how your benefits will be figured and why the unemployment office is asking about your past earnings.

If you've determined that you are eligible, then it's on to the forms. You must file an initial claim for benefits with the unemployment office. The fourth chapter, on the initial claim, carefully shows you how to fill out your form. A sample application is used to highlight every important question asked and to show you how to respond appropriately. Many people make mistakes on this first form and end up seeing their benefit check several months later instead of weeks. If you spend time on this form and understand what the questions are looking for and how to respond honestly, simply, and concisely, you will receive your check that much quicker.

If you've already filed for benefits and received a denial slip instead of money, chapter five explains how to appeal that decision. You are given an automatic right to appeal. If you are denied benefits, you will automatically receive a hearing—but you must file your form on time. Here, you will find an extensive list of tips on how to handle your appeal hearing. Since most of you will represent yourselves at these hearings, this handbook offers very detailed explanations and a check list on how to prepare, how to respond, and how to argue your case. The more prepared you are, the better you will present your side of the story to win your benefits.

Chapter six covers the emotional process that is associated with job loss. You will learn to prepare yourself for this rollercoaster ride filled with extreme highs and intense lows. A list of suggestions offers ways to handle this wide range of ups and downs.

As you ride this rollercoaster, the unemployment office expects you to search for a new job simultaneously. In this chapter, you'll find a brief rundown of the most common ways of finding a job. It also shows you which ways of searching are the most effective. Since this book is primarily about receiving your unemployment benefits, chapter six directs you to other books and resources for your job search. It also gives you information and references for managing your debt.

Other social service benefits are explained in this chapter as well. If you were injured on the job, you should look into workers' compensation. If you are injured while at home, you should consider disability benefits. These services and more are summarized in this chapter.

In the back of the book, you'll find sample forms, along with notices from the unemployment office that may be sent to you. The forms are explained and tips are offered on how to fill them out so that you can avoid the most common stumbling blocks to receiving benefits.

It has become clear that being laid off is an aspect of life, and it's time to take away the fear and anxiety, so that you can turn what is often a devastating emotional time into a personal triumph. With extra financial support through your unemployment benefits, you have a better chance of finding a new job or starting a new career that may be more rewarding than your last.

Cautionary Tale: A Woman Out of Work

Walking into work Monday morning, Meg sees another desk swept clear of last Friday's papers and of belongings. Now, twelve empty desks sit like oak tombstones in her department. For a moment, Meg wonders if she will be next. But it's unlikely, she says, comforting herself. She's worked in the customer service department for ten years. She designed the customer help manual. She's always cheerful and has trained almost every person in her department.

She settles into her chair and plugs into her station. Ten minutes later, her intercom buzzes to life. "Uh, will you come into my office?" asks her supervisor. Meg walks in and her stomach sinks. "Business is slow. It's nothing personal. But you know how it goes. It's been a great ten years." She has two weeks to pack up her belongings.

Meg walks out, a zombie paralyzed by ecstasy and shock. A new chance at something again. Ten years at one job is a long time. She could be her own boss. She has skills. But by the end of the day, she's miserable. How could they? Ten years of her life and she gets a lousy couple weeks to move on? Desperately in need of self-assurance, she calls her friend that night, who reminds her that she had been talking about getting a new job for months now. That two years ago, Meg had said that she always wanted to be an interior designer.

Meg's friend convinces her to sign up for a night class in interior design at a local community college the next day. Meg also researches the field; how much can she make, what skills will she need. She joins a women's networking group. And then someone at her job club suggests that she should file for unemployment benefits. Meg had never thought she could. Since she'd gone to college, held a good job, and saved a little money, Meg assumed that she was disqualified from any financial support. But her unemployed friend persuades her to file anyway. Unfortunately, she waits three weeks before going down to the unemployment office and filing out the forms for benefits.

Uncertain how to fill out the form, she checks the wrong box, indicating that she was terminated when she should have marked "laid off." Now, she's informed the unemployment office that she was at fault for losing her job. They will take a careful look at her application before approving it. Then, she makes another critical error: she gives a long explanation as to why she was laid off, adding information that works against her. She puts down that she's interested in becoming an interior designer and is not sure how her current skills as a customer service operator for a computer company transfer to this new field. At her unemployment benefits interview, she repeats her interest in a career change. Right then, she's told the unemployment office that she won't be available for work until she's acquired skills to make the career change. Her interviewer writes this down, noting that Meg has probably failed to meet the "available for work" criteria. Meg forgot to mention that she will continue to look for work in the computer area. She has cast a substantial amount of doubt on her application for benefits. And all she's done so far is fill out two questions on her initial form and answer one question asked by the interviewer.

Three weeks pass, and she hears nothing. She files her continued claim forms for each week that she's unemployed. Then, she receives a letter telling her that she is denied benefits. The letter says that her former employer claimed that she was fired for misconduct.

Meg is stunned. Her former supervisor told her that business was slow. She had always received excellent work performance evaluations. Unfortunately, she thought that her employer would not fight her claim for benefits.

It's two months now since Meg was laid off. She assumed she'd have a new job by now. Meg needs money. She has spent nearly all of her savings and her severance pay. Her benefits were supposed to fill in the financial gaps. In a moment of desperation, she goes down to the unemployment office and discovers that she can appeal the decision. She picks up a form to request a hearing at the unemployment office and files it, nearly missing the deadline.

A week later, she receives a notice that her appeal hearing is in two weeks at the appeals office located next to the unemployment office. She calls home and asks to borrow some money from her mother.

On the day of her hearing, Meg fails to show up early and review her unemployment file. In that file, she would have found her initial application, responses from her former employer, and notes from the interview conducted by the unemployment officer. She would have seen the mistake the interviewer made when she mentioned her interest in interior design. Meg, however, didn't know about the file. Nor did she know that she could have used a special form to get her work evaluations from her boss. Instead, she is anxious and disorganized.

The judge first turns to Meg's former employer. He must prove that she was fired for misconduct. He tells the judge that Meg showed up late several times and left a customer on hold once for ten minutes. When it's Meg's turn, she correctly points out that that was two years ago. She also mentions that she's looking for computer work.

Three weeks later, Meg receives a notice that she's won the appeal and will immediately receive her benefits, which amount to about one-half her former weekly pay check. She's delighted to discover that her benefits are backdated to the date when she first filed. However, for those three weeks that she waited before filing, she receives nothing. She still has not found a job and decides to look for anything in computers.

Her old company calls and offers her a job in the billing department for the same pay. Meg, still angry at the way they treated her, turns it down. She marks on her continued claim form that she was offered a job but turned it down. But she fails to explain that it was her old employer that offered the job, which most states don't require you to take. One week later, she receives a notice in the mail that she no longer qualifies for benefits because she failed to accept the job offer.

Outraged, Meg files another appeal. It's been almost three months now that she's been caught up in this bureaucratic nightmare and still no job. Now, she must attend another appeal hearing and state her case a second time.

Meg did a lot of things right, but too many things wrong. She joined a support group, actively began her job search, took time to evaluate her career options, and filed for benefits. She even managed her appeal hearing well enough to receive benefits. But Meg dug herself into a hole by not understanding the unemployment system. In a way, she created her own nightmare. With a little more understanding of the process, she would have received her benefit checks within three to five weeks. *The Unemployment Survival Handbook* explains Meg's wrong turns in example after example. But more importantly, it shows you what you should do to win your own unemployment benefits the first time around.

Where To Go For Help

This book refers to the states' laws that were in effect at press time. But laws change. The technical information in the benefits chapter may not be up-to-date; your state may have changed the maximum amount of weekly benefits or slightly modified the qualifying wages required for benefits. To stay current, visit your local unemployment insurance benefits office or legal aid office to ask about changes in the law.

You may also need to seek legal help if your situation is complex. This book is not a substitute for that advice. Here are some suggestions:

- Legal Aid/Services: These are programs funded by the federal government to provide free legal advice and assist low-income people.

- State Bar Association: You can call your local bar association and ask for a referral to a private attorney. Sometimes this association has special programs to help match attorneys with clients.

- Private Attorney: Most private attorneys will not be interested in your case because there is no money to be made. If you belong to a union, however, you might get help from the union's attorney.

- Law School Clinics: If there's a local law school, it may run a clinic, which provides free legal advice to residents.

Chapter 2

Eligibility Requirements

Rob Mendol tested microchips for a computer company. In November, because of escalating rents, the company decided to relocate from Chicago to a suburb. Still living in the city, Rob commuted one-and-a-half hours to work both ways. That distance is almost ten times greater than when the company was located near his home. Instead of quitting, he tried to work out another arrangement with his boss, but his superior denied his request. So for six months, Rob endured the grueling three-hour round trip drive. Around the fourth month, he noticed that he was more irritable, both at work and home. He suffered from low back pains and drank about five cups of coffee a day to keep himself awake. In the seventh month, Rob gave notice that he was quitting because the commute had become too strenuous.

Almost immediately his back felt better. He now looks forward to waking up in the morning again, even though he doesn't have a job. Rob revises his resume and looks in the newspaper for new computer jobs closer to his home. He calls up a couple of friends working in the industry and tells them he's looking for work. He also goes down to the unemployment office and files for benefits. He figures that the extra bit of money will keep him from worrying about his finances for awhile. Will he receive any benefits?

Before you rush down to the unemployment office after you lose your job or decide to quit, you need to understand the basic requirements that must be met to become eligible for benefits. As you'll learn in this chapter, the entire unemployment benefits system runs off the concept of fault. Each time a claim for benefits is filed, those processing it ask; is this person at fault for being unemployed? If they can answer "yes" to that question, that person will be denied benefits. The key to receiving benefits is to put the fault for your unemployment on someone—your employer—or something else—a slow economy— and not yourself.

In Rob's case, most states would award benefits. Rob didn't create his transportation problem, his company did by moving its headquarters. Rob tried to work it out with his employer. But ultimately the change in traveling time was drastic enough to count as a good reason to quit. If his situation sounds similar to yours, you need to find out what your state considers too long of a commute. As you'll learn in this chapter, if Rob checks the box indicating that he "voluntarily quit" and then writes "because of a work-related reason" on his initial claim form, he stands a good chance of receiving his benefits.

Whose Fault Is It?

Since the concept of fault is so crucial, here are more examples to help you determine if you are eligible. Did you repeatedly show up late for work, even though your boss gave you warnings that you would be fired if you continued? Or was business so slow that your employer had to lay off some people, including you?

When your boss fires you because of your repeated tardiness, you'll have a hard time convincing the unemployment office that you should receive benefits. You were warned that your conduct would lead to unemployment. You had a chance to change your behavior.

But it's not your fault that your employer's business is slow right now. In this case, you'd receive your benefits.

What if you are late now and then? You tell your supervisor that when your kids miss the bus, you have to drive them to school. That makes you a half-an-hour late. It happens a couple of times. Then a couple more. Your boss says nothing until one day, he calls you into his office and tells you that he has to let you go because you are unreliable.

In this case, you would most likely win your unemployment benefits. You told your boss you would be late now and then. At that moment, he had an opportunity to disapprove and give you a warning that if you continued that conduct, you would be dismissed. But he didn't. You were late, once, twice, several more times, and he didn't say anything. Then, one day, boom, you're fired.

As you can see, the facts are very important in determining whether you will win unemployment benefits.

Jobs Not Covered

Although you are most likely covered by the unemployment benefits system, some kinds of employment fall outside its scope. But even if you see your job listed here, file for benefits anyway because your employer may have voluntarily contributed to be included in the system. Or the law may have changed and an occupation that was once excluded from receiving benefits may now be included.

- Agricultural Labor: Most states give unemployment benefits to those farm employees who worked on large farms. Only five states (California, Florida, Minnesota, Rhode Island, Texas) plus Washington, D.C., Puerto Rico, and the Virgin Islands cover work performed on smaller farms.

- Domestic Worker: All states cover domestic service in private homes, college clubs, or fraternities if your quarterly wages equal or exceed $1,000. Four jurisdictions go beyond this. The District of Columbia, New York, and the Virgin Islands cover such service if the quarterly payroll is at least $500, and Hawaii includes you in its system if your employer's payroll is $225 or more.

- Service for Relative: If you are a spouse or child, you are excluded from receiving benefits if you work for your spouse or parent. But in New York, you are allowed to collect benefits if you work for your son or daughter.

- Service of Students and Spouses of Students: If you are a student, enrolled and regularly attending classes, you cannot collect benefits if you worked for your school, college, or university. If you are a student and your spouse was hired by the school primarily to give you financial aid, your unemployed spouse is also excluded.

- Service of Patients for Hospitals: If you are a patient of a hospital and worked for that hospital, you may be excluded from receiving benefits.

- Self-Employment: If you work for yourself, you are not included in the unemployment benefit system. One small exception exists in California. You may apply for self-coverage, if you have employees of your own and receive approval from the unemployment insurance benefit office.

  Many states provide special programs if your self-employment is interrupted by a disaster. If this happened to you, ask at your unemployment benefits office about disaster benefits.

  It is difficult to determine eligibility if you are self-employed. You may have several jobs, one of which is self-employment. You may be able to qualify under one of your other jobs if you become unemployed. Apply for benefits and let the unemployment office make the decision.

- Officers of Corporations: Some states have enacted exclusions from coverage and restrictions on benefits to corporate officers.

- Some Services for State and Local Government: If you come under one of the following, you may not be covered: an elected official, member of a legislative body or state judiciary; member of the state national guard or air national guard; or a temporary employee hired in case of emergencies; or a person in an advisory position.

- Paid by Commission: If you are paid only through commission (sales people, real estate agents), you are probably not covered by the unemployment system.

Remember: In all states except Alabama, Massachusetts, and New York, employers may elect to cover types of employment that are exempt under their laws. Check with your unemployment office to see if your employer has been paying unemployment taxes.

The Fundamentals of Eligibility

You need to take a close look at how and why you lost your job. Be honest with yourself about what happened, so that you can determine whether you are eligible to receive benefits and what arguments your employer might raise to keep you from getting them.

As you glance at your initial claim form, you see some words that have important legal meanings—laid off, misconduct, voluntarily quit for a good work-related reason, and voluntarily quit for a personal reason. These terms have to be handled very carefully because they serve as sirens to the unemployment benefits system as to whether you are at fault for being unemployed.

Laid Off

This is the easiest to handle. If you are laid off because business is slow and there was no work for you, you will receive benefits.

Misconduct

All state laws contain special provisions denying benefits to employees who have been discharged for misconduct. You probably have a general idea what misconduct means, but it has a legal meaning too. Although every state defines misconduct slightly differently, it usually means that you deliberately violated an important obligation owed to your employer. It's up to your employer to show that you did all four things:

- A serious violation
- Of an important obligation
- Owed to your employer
- Done deliberately.

If your employer doesn't have evidence establishing all four of these factors, you are not guilty of misconduct.

These four factors also provide you with opportunities to argue that your actions do not amount to misconduct. For example, you might be able to argue that it wasn't a serious violation of your employer's rule to show up for work three minutes late four days in a row. And when your employer told you to type up his ten letters by five o'clock, and it took you a day-and-a-half longer, this wasn't an important obligation owed to your employer. The letters were mailed and your employer didn't lose any business.

As you weigh whether your actions amounted to misconduct, here are some things you should consider.

- Deliberate or Intentional Action: Probably the most important of the factors listed above is number four: did you act deliberately? What distinguishes misconduct from other kinds of behavior is that you must have had some control over the situation and that your actions show that you intentionally went against your obligations to your employer. You knew that what you were doing would hurt your employer's business, but you did it anyway.

  For example, stealing property from your employer or lying on your time sheet are intentional acts, done with full awareness of your actions. (Although in chapter five on winning your appeal, there may be arguments that you can present to defend yourself.)

  Misconduct is not just intentionally breaking a law. It can also be intentionally violating your employer's rules. If you consistently interfere with other people's work or if you violate reasonable working rules, such as constantly showing up late, these actions are also considered misconduct for which you can be denied benefits.

- Reasonable Rule: Your employer's rule, however, must be reasonable, fair, and enforced uniformly. If the rule is not enforced uniformly, you may have been discriminated against. Be sure to read the brief summary of discrimination in chapter four.

- Carelessness Isn't Misconduct: Carelessness and poor work performance typically are not considered misconduct. Examples of acting careless or incompetently include dropping something, forgetting to do something, using poor judgment, or lacking skills to do your job properly. But acting carelessly or incompetently can amount to misconduct if the number of incidents are great enough or your employer's business is seriously damaged. For example, a bank teller may be disqualified from receiving benefits if he repeatedly failed to balance his accounts.

- Misconduct Connected to Work: In most cases, your misconduct must be connected with your employer's work. Often, that means that your actions must have occurred at your workplace or you must have used company equipment. Sometimes an employee's personal conduct will affect his eligibility for benefits. In a recent case, a school janitor was denied unemployment benefits because he was convicted of child abuse, even though he committed the crime while off work and off school grounds.

- Time Factor: Your discharge must be the result of the alleged misconduct. If you showed up late for work for a month and then one year later, your employer fires you for misconduct, you will receive your benefits, because too much time passed between your misconduct and your firing.

Common Charges of Misconduct

Below are some common forms of misconduct: insubordination, excessive tardiness and absenteeism, intoxication, and dishonesty. Read the following descriptions to determine whether your employer's charges of misconduct are justified.

- Insubordination: If you disobey your employer, argue with your superiors, or exceed your authority, you've acted with insubordination. To be guilty of insubordination, you must have intentionally gone against your employer's orders. If you didn't know about a particular rule—that your lunch break was thirty minutes because everyone always took an hour and your employer never made it clear—then you didn't intentionally act against your employer when you, too, had an hour lunch break.

  Typically, the unemployment office looks for cumulative behavior that establishes a pattern of insubordination: you are always late, you always swear at your superior, or, when you are told to do something a certain way, you almost always do it another way. Even if there is a pattern, most often the unemployment office tries to determine if your employer gave you warnings or some notice that you would be fired if you continued. But if your one-time act of insubordination substantially harms the employer—you blow up the factory, or forget to turn the security alarm on and everything is stolen—you won't receive your benefits.

  If your employer's request is unreasonable—asking you to illegally spy on a competitor or to infiltrate a competitor's company—your refusal to comply is not misconduct.

- Tardiness/Absences: Frequent absences from work without a good reason may be considered misconduct, especially if you fail to tell your employer that you will be gone and your employer has warned you that this conduct will lead to dismissal.

  But just because you're late or absent doesn't mean it's misconduct. Here are some examples that most likely won't be considered misconduct: an isolated instance of being absent from work; an absence from work due to causes over which you have no control; repeated absences or tardiness, but your employer does not give a reprimand or warning of dismissal.

- Intoxication on the Job: Drinking on the job usually qualifies as misconduct. But if you are an alcoholic and cannot control your drinking, you may not be guilty of misconduct. Factors that will be considered by the unemployment office include: the frequency of your drunkenness at work, whether you were reprimanded, and whether the reprimands included threats of dismissal.

- Dishonesty: A knowing falsehood or misrepresentation to your employer concerning your work constitutes misconduct. False statements, including those on your employment application, may be acts of misconduct, particularly if you are in a position requiring trustworthiness. For example, a newspaper reporter who failed to tell her employer of an error in her article, and then misrepresented the date upon which she discovered the error, was denied benefits because of her misconduct.

More Examples of Misconduct

Here are more complicated cases where the employees were charged by the employers with misconduct. In some of these examples, the employee was able to argue that his conduct was not misconduct.

- Dan worked as a cook for three years at a convalescent center. He started spreading rumors that the boss was fooling around with one of the staff. At the same time, he was helping organize a union. In his last year, many complaints about his poor cooking were filed with the employer. Dan's employer discharged him for misconduct. Will he get his benefits?

Dan tried to argue that he was discharged because of his union activities. That might have worked, since there are laws that protect union organizers. But here Dan failed to have any evidence that this was so. The unemployment office found that he was intentionally trying to hurt the employer's business by spreading untrue rumors. He was denied benefits.

- Ray worked as a senior auto body repairman for three years. On four separate days, he took an excessive amount of time to complete his work. Each day his employer gave him a warning to shape up or be fired. Instead, Ray continued talking on the phone and with other employees instead of working. He was fired for misconduct.

  Ray didn't receive his benefits. His pattern of a poor attitude and specific actions that damaged his employer's business were found to be misconduct. The court emphasized the warnings he received from his employer.

- Elaine was talking in the cafeteria with another employee whose car was towed from the employer's parking lot because it didn't have the right permit. Elaine said that if that happened to her, she'd put a bomb in the back seat of the employee relations manager's car. The floor monitor overheard her and called her into the office. Elaine's employer had received bomb threats in the past and the floor monitor took Elaine's comment seriously. Elaine was fired for misconduct.

  But Elaine was able to argue that her comment was just a joke. It was said in a cafeteria, in a relaxed atmosphere. Her boss was nowhere nearby. And her employer failed to show any evidence of a relationship between her comment and previous bomb threats.

- Bill worked nine years as an exhaust pipe bender. He started talking with other employees about starting his own company and asked them to join him. He went to a bank to see about a loan. Bill was fired for trying to compete with his employer.

  Even though Bill did very good work, the unemployment office found that he was fired for misconduct. He was intentionally hurting his employer's business by soliciting other employees. He was denied benefits.

- Melody failed to reveal her prior surgery for carpal tunnel syndrome on her job application for a newspaper reporter position. She was fired for misconduct and didn't receive benefits because her lie meant that she couldn't effectively do the work she was hired to do.

- Dana worked as a stripper and was eventually moved to a more prominent time slot. She didn't receive an increase in pay, but she did get more health benefits. She worked for a month, and then refused to perform unless she was paid more.

  She was denied benefits because the unemployment office found that her employer's request for her to perform at the designated time was a reasonable one. She had agreed to the terms of the new job at the time she accepted the promotion.

- As a packer for the last twenty years, Fred only occasionally drove the company's storage trucks and delivered customer's boxes. His usual job, however, was packing the storage boxes. During one trip, he drove the truck into an underpass and ripped off the top after miscalculating the size of the truck. Fred's accident resulted in $4,000 in damages. He was fired for misconduct.

  Fred's actions did not amount to misconduct. He had no intention of hurting his employer's business and this was his first accident in twenty years.

- Donna worked as a checker and supervised other checkers at a grocery store. All employees belonged to a union. On two different occasions, Donna yelled at employees in front of customers for not quitting their shift on time and violating union rules. She also humiliated both employees, making customers feel uncomfortable. She was fired.

  She did not receive benefits because she knew that her conduct hurt her employer's business. After the first outburst, her employer had warned her never to yell in front of customers.

Labor Union Strike

If you go on strike or there is a lockout, in most instances you will not receive benefits.

Some states will give you benefits if there is a lockout and you have no choice but not to work, or if the dispute results from the employer not adhering to the law on wages, hours, working conditions, or collective bargaining, or if the employees protest substandard working conditions.

This is a complicated area of the law and you should to talk with your union attorney, a private attorney, or a legal aid attorney.

You Voluntarily Quit Your Job

If you decide to quit your job, you can still receive benefits if you had a good reason, or as most states say, a "good cause" for leaving your work. The majority of states require that the good cause have something to do with your work. But some states allow you to quit for a personal reason as well. If your employer tells you that he will soon be laying you off because business is slow, don't quit. It's much easier to receive your benefits if you wait for your employer to lay you off. Even if he threatens to fire you, don't resign. It's up to your employer to jump through hoops and show that he fired you because of misconduct. If he doesn't do a good job of convincing the unemployment office of this, you'll receive your benefits. But if you quit your job, it is up to you to establish good cause.

"Good cause" has a legal meaning. Here, it typically refers to a serious and compelling problem that you've tried to work out with your employer, but have been unable to solve. For example, you've talked with your employer about a leave of absence or a change in your work conditions, because the cigarette smoke is aggravating your asthma. Or you've asked if there are other jobs available within the company, because staring at a computer screen for eight hours a day is giving you terrible migraines. The work-related problem keeps you from working, even though you'd like to work.

Even if you have a good cause for quitting, be prepared for your former employer to tell the unemployment office that he discharged you because of misconduct or you left without a good cause. Your employer is trying to save himself money. Each time another former employee qualifies for benefits, your employer must pay higher taxes.

Work-Related Reasons

Here are some examples of good cause that have been used before to voluntarily quit a job and still receive benefits.

- Illegal Job Requests: Your employer asks you to perform an illegal act—stealing trade secrets from a competitor or participating in a price-fixing scheme. As you'll read in the fifth chapter, this allegation is difficult to prove, since it's most often your word against your employer's. Try and think of other evidence that supports your story such as a memo or other coworkers asked to do the same thing.

- Illegal Working Conditions: If you are asked to work in conditions that threaten your health and safety, you may have a good cause to leave. Hopefully, before you quit your job, you brought the condition to your employer's attention. Try to remember the date that you told your employer, because the unemployment agent who interviews you should know this. Make sure that you've documented the health risk by going to see a doctor. Have the doctor write up his recommendation that you quit your job because of health reasons.

- Injury on the Job: If you are injured at work, you should find out about workers' compensation. (See chapter six for a brief description). If you're not clear which you should file for, unemployment benefits or workers' compensation, file for both and let the two offices decide which benefit is appropriate for you.

  If you qualify for workers' compensation, you often can collect unemployment benefits when your workers' compensation ends.

- Broken Promises: If you were hired with your employer's promise for more pay, a promotion, or a lateral move, and the promise never materializes, you may have good cause to voluntarily quit your job and still receive benefits. Ideally, this promise was made in writing; otherwise, it's your word against your employer's. At your interview with the unemployment agent, be ready to explain the promise and how it influenced your decision to work there. Explain how it was broken and how you were injured by this.

- Major Changes in Your Job: Major changes in your job—duties, wages, hours, conditions, transportation—may provide a good cause. You'll need to research how drastic the change needs to be to qualify for benefits. You can look up past decisions made by the appeals board to find out how your state rules on this issue. See chapter five about conducting this research.

- Intolerable Conditions: Examples of intolerable conditions include sexual harassment, discrimination, and repeated use of offensive language. Again, this one will be a tough situation to prove, since it's most

often your word against your employer's. Try and think of other evidence that supports your position—other coworkers, documents, or comments made in the past by your employer.

- Personal Health Reasons: When work conditions endanger your health, you may have a good cause for leaving. At your interview, explain what your duties were, how they changed, and how your health was harmed. If it's true, explain that you told your boss about the problems and he failed to do anything to change the situation. You should have documentation from a doctor as to how your working conditions aggravated or caused your illness.

  Where an injury or illness is severe enough to compel you to leave work, that same physical condition may also prevent you from being "able and available" for work. As explained later in this chapter, you need to show that although your work conditions caused or aggravated your illness, you are still able to do other work.

- Hours/Wages: Unduly long hours are generally considered good cause for leaving, especially where the hours adversely affect your health. You also may have good cause if your wages were substantially reduced or your full-time work was reduced to part-time; or if your wages were substantially less than the prevailing wage rate in your community for your kind of work (or below union wage rate, if you are a member of the union) and you left as soon as you discovered the difference.

Summary of Voluntary Quit

If you voluntarily quit your job, you must convince the unemployment office that:

1. A problem existed at work or at home (depending on the state).

2. The problem was serious and

3. You tried to work the problem out with your employer: you told your employer about the problem; you requested a job change;

4. Or there was no point in notifying your employer because other employees have tried to change it and he hasn't responded.

Personal Reasons for Quitting

Many states grant benefits to you even if you quit for a personal reason unrelated to work. Those states include: Alaska, California, Hawaii, Nebraska, Nevada, New York, Ohio, Oregon, Pennsylvania, Rhode Island, South Carolina, Utah, Virginia, and the dependencies of Puerto Rico and the Virgin Islands. Some states not listed here will give you benefits if you become ill or if your personal reason is compelling. So even if your state is not listed here, file anyway, because you may be able to argue that your personal situation fits one of the exceptions in your state. The following is a list of personal reasons that were used in past cases and resulted in benefits.

- Moving: If your spouse or soon-to-be spouse is offered a new job in a different city and you have to quit your job to stay together, your state may accept this reason. But before you quit, check to see if your employer has an office in the new city and would consider transferring you there.

- Caring for a Relative or Child: You may have a good cause for leaving your work if a family member becomes sick, and there is no one else to take care of her. Before you quit, check to see if your employer would grant you a leave of absence from your job. If your employer agrees, get it in writing. In most states, if you are on leave, you cannot collect unemployment benefits. If your employer does not have a leave of absence policy, be ready to show this to the unemployment agent. Your company policy may be written down in an employee manual.

- Retirement: If you leave your job because of compulsory retirement provisions of a pension, retirement, collective bargaining contract, or an employer policy, a majority of states will give you benefits on the theory that your leaving is involuntary.

- Pregnancy: Most states deny you benefits if you leave work because of pregnancy. However, if you leave based on your doctor's advice and are able and available to do other kinds of work, many states will give you benefits.

- Religion: If your religious beliefs are violated by your work, you may have good cause to quit, but only if you didn't know that the job would violate your religion when you originally took it.

- Illness: If you become ill, you may still be able to collect unemployment or disability benefits in some states. Those states that offer disability benefits include: New York, California, Hawaii, Rhode Island and New Jersey and the dependency of Puerto Rico. Typically, these states require you to submit a doctor's medical file, inform your employer, ask for a leave of absence, and return to your job when you are better. You may also be able to collect welfare benefits, depending on your income level, as well as food stamps. For more information, see chapter six.

Examples of Voluntarily Quitting With Good Cause

- Jane left her job to go back to school full time. She applied for unemployment benefits. Will she receive them? In most cases, this would not constitute a good cause for leaving your job.

- Joe, a restaurant chef, was subjected to numerous derogatory racial remarks from his employer, coworkers, and even patrons of the restaurant. Instead of continuing to endure the discriminatory behavior of his employer, Joe decided to quit. Should he receive benefits? Yes. Although discrimination is difficult to prove, often requiring witnesses and documentation, quitting because of discrimination is a good cause.

- Jim, a lumberman, had worked at the mill for fifteen years. Now sixty years old, he noticed that he became short of breath while working at the chip-making machine. He went to see his doctor, who told him that his work was too strenuous and he should quit or risk more serious health problems. With a written medical record of his condition, Jim quit his job. Should he receive benefits? Yes. Jim has the necessary paperwork to show that his job was harming his health.

- While working as a receptionist at a law firm, Alice decided to look for more exciting work. She interviewed with several investment firms for a financial analyst position and eventually received a firm offer of employment. Alice gave notice and quit her job. In the meantime, however, her new employer decided that he no longer needed a new analyst. Will Alice be able to receive benefits? Yes; in most states, if you leave work to accept a new job, and the new job is then unavailable, you are eligible for benefits.

Able to Work and Available for Work

In addition to showing the unemployment office that you had a good cause for leaving your job or that you were laid off, you must also establish that you are able and available for work, either in your typical line of business or in some other position that reasonably matches your education and training. For each week that you are unemployed, you must meet the "able and available for work" requirement. Some states require you to file a "continued claim" form for each week (or every two weeks) that you are unemployed. On that form, there will be questions asking about your availability and your ability to work (See Appendix, for a sample form).

How to Show You Are Able and Available

- **Registering for Work:** Although registering for work at the employment office located at or near the unemployment office is some indication that you are available, you typically have to do more than that. All states require you to register for work and report to the office, usually once a week. In most states, if you don't respond to letters and other messages from the employment office relating to a job opening, you are not complying with reporting requirements. The only way to avoid being ineligible at that point is to present a good reason for not responding. Some of the reasons that have worked in the past include coercion from your employer, misleading statements from an unemployment agent, or circumstances beyond your control.

- **Job Search:** In addition to registering, most states require that you begin an active job search. If you use some of the job search techniques described in chapter six, you will show that you are available for work.

- **Few Restrictions:** If you place too many restrictions upon the kind of work or workplace conditions—distance you will travel, wages, hours, tasks—that you will accept, you will most likely be considered "unavailable" for work. In a sense, you've defined your universe of acceptable jobs so narrowly that there is no job market available for you.

  For example, if you decide to take a course at the local community college during your mornings, you've made yourself unavailable for most eight-hour jobs. However, if you were a night-time security guard at your

last job and there are openings for you to do that job again, you may be considered available for work and eligible to receive benefits. The unemployment agent who interviews you about your claim (see chapter four about the interview) may point out that you've put too many restrictions on your availability. Take this person's advice and revise your request for $40,000 if you only earned $25,000 in your last job.

When you're filling out your unemployment benefits form, you will be asked about the wage and hours you want at your next job. A good rule of thumb is to write in figures that are similar to your last job, unless you've moved and the wages are different in that area. Chapter four explains how to fill out your initial claim.

Examples of Able and Available

- Training Course: If you've enrolled in a training course that is approved by your unemployment office, you are still considered able and available for work. Generally, the unemployment office will approve your training program if it's limited to vocational or basic education training. Check with your local community college for approved courses.

- Move: If you have to move to a new location, it is generally not necessary that a specific job opening exists for you, but you should be able to show that your chances of getting a job in your new area are about the same as those in your old location.

- Health Problems: If you voluntarily quit due to health problems and those problems were considered good cause for leaving, those same health problems could prevent you from being available for work. However, if you establish that you can work in a number of other jobs, you are able and available for work.

  Another example where your good cause reason may lead to a denial of benefits because you are not available is when you must care for a child or relative. If you search for someone to take care of your child during a summer break, but have no luck, you may choose to quit your job. If you can show that you are available a reasonable amount of time (you can't work the night shift, but you can work the morning or afternoon shift), this will help convince the unemployment office that you are available for work. But remember, before you decide to quit, ask your employer for a leave of absence from your job.

- Pregnancy: If you are pregnant and leave your job, you must show that you are able to work, actively seeking work, and unable to find work in order to collect benefits.

- Appearance: In some areas of the country, the way you dress and wear your hair may determine whether you are available for work.

Accepting Suitable Work

You've begun your job search, contacting friends, going on informational interviews, and using governmental job search services. You've sent out resumes and follow-up thank you letters. You've received a couple of nibbles, and then, you get the call. A job offer. You listen to what your hours will be and your responsibilities. It sounds good. You're ready to take the offer, but then you hear what they'd like to pay you. You've done your research and know that what they're offering is substantially less than the market price. So you decline the offer and forge ahead with your search, continuing to receive benefits.

Although you have to search actively for a job and be available for employment, you don't have to take any job that comes along. Your physical fitness, training, earnings, and experience determine the suitability of a job. Every state says that the job offered to you is not suitable if:

(1) it is available because of a strike, lockout, or other labor dispute;

(2) the wages, hours, or conditions of the job are substantially less favorable than those prevailing for similar work in the community; or

(3) you would be required to join a union or resign from a union.

If you interview for a job and find out that any of these three conditions exist, you can refuse the job for that reason and still receive your benefits.

Many states also include those things that qualify as a good cause for you to leave your last job. For example, if the job poses a risk to your health, safety, or morals, or the distance from your home is too far, your unemployment office will most likely agree with you that the job is unsuitable. The longer you are out of job, however, the less willing the unemployment office will grant you these good causes for refusing an offer.

Examples of Unsuitable Work

- A bona fide job offer: Before you even get to the question of suitability, the job offer has to be just that, an offer. If the offer is vague, lacking in detail as to the type of work, wage rate, or hours, you most likely did not receive a genuine offer. So if you rejected it, you will still receive benefits.

- Religion: If you are offered a job, but it requires you to work on Sundays, which violates your religious beliefs, most states would say the job is unsuitable and you would still qualify for benefits.

- Distance: You were laid off from your job as a store window designer in Los Angeles and decided to move to New York to find another job. With the last box unpacked, your old employer calls you and offers your old job back. You refuse. You will still receive your benefits because the distance is too far to make it suitable work for you.

- Not physically able: If you left your job as a construction worker because you injured your back, you don't have to accept another construction position, as long as you have other skills, such as selling goods, accounting, or bookkeeping, that will qualify you for a job. Remember: The longer you are unemployed, the less particular you can be about accepting a job offer.

Fraud

If you use fraudulent means to receive your benefits—lying on your initial claim form, or making an agreement with your employer—you may have to repay the benefits or have them deducted from future benefits. You could also be fined and imprisoned. All of the arguments presented here for how and why you lost or quit your job are based on the premise that you will use them only if they are true.

If You Are Denied Benefits

As you've seen, the three major ways to be denied benefits are being discharged for misconduct, voluntarily quitting your job without a good reason, and refusing to take suitable work. Less common is disqualification for misrepresentation to obtain benefits. When you are denied benefits, you are considered disqualified from receiving this money. Unlike being unavailable for work or unable to work, which ends as soon as your condition changes, disqualification means that your benefits are denied for a definite period of time.

The disqualification imposed for these causes varies considerably among the states. They may include one or a combination of the following:

1. A postponement of benefits for a certain period of time: You are denied benefits for several weeks. Then, if you still haven't been able to find a job, you can reapply for benefits.

2. A cancellation of benefits: Most states using this method require you to earn a certain amount of wages at a new job before you can collect benefits. Typically, you have to earn a specific ratio of the benefits that you would have gotten had you qualified the first time around. There's a way around this requirement, however.

If you've figured out that you aren't eligible for benefits, don't rush down to the unemployment office because you will be denied benefits. Instead, try and find a short-term job. When you are laid off from this work, then go down and apply for benefits. This way, your eligibility is determined based on this last short-term job. In this case, because you were laid off, you will receive your benefits.

How Your Benefits Calculation Determines Your Eligibility

In addition to fault and whether you've rejected a suitable job offer, the manner in which benefits are calculated determines your eligibility. In chapter three on benefits, you will learn that you need to have earned a certain amount of money or worked a specified length of time or both to qualify. This is called your "qualifying wages and hours."

Why Your Employer Will Fight Your Claim

Even if you meet all the criteria and are eligible for benefits, you should prepare your initial filing as if your employer will fight it. This is the most realistic approach to filing for benefits, because employers look for ways to cut costs, one of those being your unemployment benefits.

When you file for benefits, your employer doesn't pay them directly to you. She pays these benefits indirectly. Each employer that is covered by the system pays a tax that goes into a special state fund to pay for benefits.

Employers hold a financial interest in preventing you from receiving benefits. In most states (except Alaska, New Jersey, and Pennsylvania, which also collect employee contributions), employers pay taxes into a fund, and these payments are not deducted from the employee's wages. As the number of employees collecting benefits increases, so does the tax rate. This rising cost provides an incentive for the employer to characterize the facts surrounding your job loss as your fault, no matter what actually happened, so that you will be denied benefits. This fact should prepare you for a potential fight and should remind you to review chapter four about filing your initial claim carefully, so that you don't make a mistake and invite a denial of benefits.

Benefits: How Much Do You Get?

Chapter 3

C arol, a former film developer, makes a quick calculation on the inside margin of her book. With her rent, living expenses, and money set aside for emergencies, she needs a minimum of $1,200 a month. She's got some savings stashed away and another paycheck coming. She will hold a garage sale and get rid of all the junk in her basement. She will look into a part-time job, teaching Italian to students from her home, but only if it doesn't affect her benefits dramatically. She makes a note to ask someone about this.

She scribbles some more numbers in the margin and figures out how much she needs from her unemployment check. Seeing this dollar figure, Carol becomes concerned: will she get that amount? How much will her benefits be? What if it isn't enough? From whom could she borrow money? She reaches for her small book of telephone numbers and wonders who still owes her money and how she could collect. She jots a couple names down, adds her parents at the top of the list.

Maybe she should move to a cheaper apartment. But she'd hate to pack and leave her garden, hardwood floors, and early morning sunlight. There's been enough trauma in her life. She doesn't want to add to it the pressure of moving.

Instead, she picks up the unemployment benefit claim form and looks at the questions. She flips through the pages of the small claimant's pamphlet that she found at the unemployment office. She frantically searches for how much her benefits will be. Nothing seems to make sense: base period, weekly benefit amount, waiting period. She could have handled this jargon if she weren't so tense from having lost her job. But now, she lacks the patience to read the fine print carefully. Dazed, she sets down the forms and decides to file next week instead.

Before going any farther, I'm going to explain some of the terminology used by unemployment benefits offices to determine whether you qualify for benefits and to figure out your benefit amount. After you've briefly familiarized yourself with this jargon, turn to page 49. Here, you will find a state-by-state chart that gives you everything you need to know to determine whether you've worked long enough and made enough money to qualify for benefits. You will also find on this chart the method that your state uses to figure out the amount of your weekly benefit check. When needed, you should refer back to the terminology section in this chapter to be certain you understand the chart.

It's important for you to determine whether you have the necessary wages and hours, so that you don't file your claim and have it denied. But it's not crucial that you know the exact figure of your weekly benefit amount. If you abhor math, you can skip that part and figure that you will receive roughly 50 percent of your highest weekly wage amount for about twenty-six weeks. This estimate can be used in your budget. (See chapter six on designing a budget.)

If you don't mind a little math, you can figure out the best time to file and maximize the amount of money you receive each week from the unemployment benefits office. As you'll see in this chapter, the date you decide to file can have a significant effect on how much money you will receive.

Your Base Period

Your unemployment office determines whether you are eligible for benefits and calculates your benefit amount by taking a specific period of time from your past and looking at what you were doing in terms of work. They scrutinize the kind of job that you held and how much money you made and sometimes how many hours you worked. This specific period is called the *base period* and it typically runs one year—fifty-two weeks. If you did not work at all during this period of time, you won't qualify for benefits. But you aren't required to have worked the full fifty-two weeks and you need not have held the same job during that time to receive benefits. You could have worked three jobs in several different states and still be able to collect benefits. You also may have worked consecutive months (January through June) or nonconsecutive and still qualify for benefits.

If you did work during this time, the job(s) must have been one covered by the unemployment insurance benefit system. (See chapter two for those jobs that don't fall within the unemployment system.) Whatever jobs you held, the wages that you earned during this time period determine your total benefits. You will read about this in the weekly benefit amount section of this chapter.

Methods of Determining Your Base Period

Whether you are trying to figure out if you qualify for benefits or how much money you can get, you need to understand how your state determines your base period. Almost all of the states determine the base period in one of four different ways. And every state's method for defining the base period relies on the date when you apply for benefits. From that date, the unemployment office looks back in time to see what you earned and how long you worked.

Many of the states use calendar quarters to define the parameters of the base period. You will see in the following description that the majority of states define their base period as the first four of the last five quarters. A quarter is three months long, so there are four calendar quarters in one year. The first quarter of a calendar year runs from January 1 until March 30, the second quarter runs from April 1 to June 30, the third quarter is July 1 to September 30, and the final quarter is from October 1 until December 31.

First Type of Base Period: Your base period is the fifty-two weeks immediately prior to your filing a claim. If you filed on October 1, 1993, your base period would run from September 30, 1992 until September 30, 1993. The states utilizing this method of determination include Massachusetts and Michigan. In New York, there's a one week lag between when you file a valid claim and when your base period ends.

Second Type of Base Period: Your base period is the last four completed calendar quarters prior to the date of filing your claim. If you filed on October 1, 1993, the last four quarters begin with October 1, 1992 and run until the fourth quarter ending September 30, 1993—twelve months from the time you filed. Remember to think of completed calendar quarters. For example, if you filed on November 1, 1993, you would still start your base period on October 1, 1992 and run it to September 30, 1993. The four completed quarters would be: the first quarter, ending December 31, 1992, the second quarter, running until March 31, the third, ending June 30 and the last completed quarter, ending September 30, 1993. Nebraska uses this model, but the state legislature is considering changing it to the third model. In Vermont, if you fail to meet the qualifying wage requirement, you can use this model instead to try and qualify.

Third Type of Base Period: The majority of states use this method. Your base period is the first four of the last five completed calendar quarters prior to when you filed your claim. So if you filed your claim on October 1, 1993, your base period starts on July 1, 1992 and runs until June 30, 1993. You need to go back one year and three months, at a minimum, to determine your base period. If your state is not listed in the other models, then it uses this one.

Fourth Type of Base Period: California uses a base period which is the first four of the last five completed calendar quarters, plus one month. So if you filed October 1, 1993, your base period begins April 1, 1992 and ends March 31, 1993.

New Hampshire uses a uniform base period, April 1 through March 31, for all valid claims. So if you file between July 1, 1992 and June 30, 1993, your base period is April 1, 1991 to March 31, 1992.

To figure out your base period, take out a piece of paper and write today's date on it. If you live in Massachusetts, it's easy—your base period ended yesterday. In those last fifty-two weeks, you must have worked and made a certain amount of money to qualify for benefits. This time period will also determine your weekly benefit amount.

If you live in a state such as Alabama, which uses the first four of the last five completed calendar quarters prior to the date of filing your valid claim, count back fifteen months from today. Wherever that fifteenth month falls, determine which quarter it falls in—the quarter ending March 31, the one ending June 30, the third one ending September 30, or the last one ending on December 31. Whatever quarter it falls into, that is your starting quarter. Now add three quarters to that and you've got your base period.

Examples of Base Periods

- Marci worked ten weeks in one state and ten weeks in another state. Both states require at least twenty weeks of work to qualify for benefits. Does Marci qualify for benefits?

  Marci qualifies in each state since the law allows her to combine her weeks for a total of twenty weeks that she worked during her base period. She can choose which state she'd like to file her claim.

- Pete worked for eighteen weeks, then was laid off because business was slow. His state requires twenty weeks of work to qualify for benefits. Instead of filing for benefits and being denied, Pete finds a part-time job and works two more weeks. He then goes to the unemployment office and files a claim. Does he qualify?

  Yes. Pete may receive a smaller benefit check because he earned income from a part-time job, rather than a full-time one, but he did the right thing in waiting to file his claim until he had the required twenty weeks.

When You Have the Advantage

Your employer during your base period may be different from your most recent employer. If that's the case, your base period employer pays for the benefits—the money is drawn from this employer's reserve account and his taxes are raised as a result. But it's your most recent employer, the one who laid you off or who fired you, who has the legal right to challenge your claim for benefits.

This situation can work in your favor. For example, if you were fired for misconduct, you would not qualify for benefits (see chapter two about eligibility). But if you are able to get another short-term job after this, and then be laid off, you will qualify for benefits. And the first employer who fired you—your base period employer—will have to pay.

Qualifying Wages and Hours

During your base period, you must have earned a certain amount of wages or worked a certain number of hours, or both, to qualify for benefits. If you don't meet your state's requirements, you're out of luck—no benefits.

Each state has a slightly different way to determine your qualifying wage, although most look at your highest quarter of earnings—the three-month period of time when you made the most money—and require that your total base period wages be a multiple of that amount. For example, you're eligible for benefits if your total base period wages amount to at least one-and-one-half times the wages received in the highest quarter. In some states, your total base wages must be one-and-one-quarter of your highest quarter of wages. Wages mean income that is actually paid to you, not wages that you earned and will be paid later. If you work in April, but are not paid until August, that income will be included in August's total, not April.

The reason your unemployment office bothers with a qualifying wage is to make sure that you regularly worked and were part of the labor force. They use a multiple of your highest quarter of earnings to make sure that your wages are spread out over the year, rather than clumped up in a one month period of time.

For example:

Base Period: (regardless of which method you use)

Quarter 1	Quarter 2	Quarter 3	Quarter 4
$2,000	0	$1,000	0

The first quarter is your high quarter of earnings. Quarters 2, 3, 4 equal one-half of your highest quarter of earnings. And your total base wages equal one-and-one-half times your high quarter earnings. If your state required this amount of wages, you'd be eligible for benefits.

If you don't meet your state's requirements, you still may be able to receive benefits. You may be able to find new employment—a part-time or temporary job—and when you are laid off or quit with good cause, you include these additional wages into the calculation for benefits. Or your state or dependency may provide less benefits to you, even though you don't quite meet the qualifying wages. (Maryland, Pennsylvania, Delaware, and Puerto Rico).

Qualifying Hours

The following eight states require you to have worked a certain number of weeks during your base period to collect benefits as well as to have made a certain amount of money:

Florida: 20 weeks
Michigan: 20 weeks*
Minnesota: 15 weeks
New Jersey: 20 weeks
New York: 20 weeks**
Ohio: 20 weeks
Oregon: 18 weeks
Washington: 680 hours***

* If you didn't work twenty weeks, Michigan allows you to qualify anyway if you have fourteen weeks of employment and wages equal to twenty times the state average weekly wage.
** You can still qualify, if you worked fifteen weeks during your base period and forty weeks preceding your base year.
*** Washington does not have any wage requirement.

Examples of Qualifying Wages and Hours

- Samantha worked full time as a check-out clerk and part time on the weekends cleaning house for two neighbors. In her state, domestic workers are not covered by the unemployment benefit system unless they make a certain amount of money. In this case, Sam didn't earn that amount. Will the wages from this part-time job be included as part of her base wages to determine if she qualified for benefits? No. Payments from exempt employers are not included. (See chapter two on eligibility to determine which jobs are not covered by the unemployment benefits system).

- John was laid off from work. But his employer had agreed to help pay for inpatient chemical dependency treatment for his alcoholism through the employer's group health insurance plan. Is John's base period extended to include his treatment since his former employer is helping to pay?

  In most states, no. In a recent case, the court decided that a worker's employment ended when he was officially laid off. These extra weeks could not be included as part of his employment.

Calculating Your Weekly Benefit Amount

Your benefit check will be roughly one-half of what you used to earn each week. In some states it will be a little more, in others, a little less. And as you'll read in this chapter, each state puts a minimum and maximum limit on how much your check will be. The big question is how much did you earn if your income varied over the year?

Some states will only look at the time you were doing your best, making the most money during a three month period of time, called your highest quarter of earnings. Other states take an average of what your weekly wage used to be. And finally, some states consider the total amount of wages you earned during your benefit year.

The calculation of your weekly benefit amount occurs in two steps. The first step is determining how much you earned during your highest quarter of earnings, or your total earnings during your base year, or your average weekly wage, depending on your state. I call this your *base wage*. Although no state officially uses this term, it may make the calculation easier to understand. The second step of the calculation is to take slightly less or slightly more than one-half of your base wage, depending on your state.

Each state varies in both these steps. Here is a breakdown of the three methods of figuring your base wage and the states that use that method. After reading this section, skip to the state-by-state chart that starts on page 49 and figure out your own weekly benefit amount.

- Highest Quarter of Earnings Method: Alabama, Arizona, Arkansas, California, Colorado, Connecticut, Washington, D.C., Delaware, Georgia, Hawaii, Idaho, Illinois, Indiana, Iowa, Kansas, Louisiana, Maine, Maryland, Massachusetts, Minnesota, Mississippi, Missouri, Nebraska, Nevada, New Mexico, North Carolina, North Dakota, Oklahoma, Pennsylvania, Puerto Rico, Rhode Island, South Carolina, South Dakota, Tennessee, Texas, Utah, Vermont, Virgin Islands, Virginia, Washington, Wisconsin, and Wyoming.

- Average Weekly Wage Method: Florida, Michigan, New Jersey, New York, and Ohio.

- Total Wages Method: Alaska, Kentucky, Montana, New Hampshire, Oregon, and West Virginia.

Example of a Benefit Calculation

Here's an example of a weekly benefit calculation using each of the three methods of base wage to show how there might be slight variations between the states' benefit check amounts.

Lance worked twenty-six weeks for $500 a week. Then he got a raise to $700 a week and worked another twenty-six weeks. He was then laid off. All fifty-two weeks of work are in his base period.

- Highest Quarter of Earnings Method: If Lance's state defines his base wages as his high quarter of earnings to compute benefits, his weekly benefits will be based on the $9,100 ($700 times thirteen weeks) that he earned in his high quarter of earnings. If he then divides by twenty-six, Lance will receive $350 a week in benefits, if his state pays that much.

- Average Weekly Wage Method: If his state uses an average weekly wage method, his average weekly wage was $600 ($500 plus $700 divided by two is $600). He will then multiply his base wage by 50 percent to figure out his weekly benefit amount, which comes to $300 ($600 times .50 is $300).

- Total Wage Method: If Lance's state uses total base wages, his benefits will be based on an annual wage of $31,200. Then, he would multiply by a certain amount, say .01185 percent if he lived in Kentucky, and find that he could receive $369 in benefits a week.

Increasing Your Benefit Amount

The unemployment office uses your wages earned during the base period to determine how much your benefits will be. Your wages can come from part-time work or full-time work, temp jobs, night shifts, or more than one job. The more wages earned in the base period, the higher the benefits, at least to a certain maximum amount.

Depending on your state's formula, one way to increase the level of your benefits is to wait to include months in your base period when you were paid a lot of money. For example, if you worked in New York and during the last week of your job, you made an extra $1,000 from a client, you should wait one week before filing, because that last week would be included in your base year and thus your benefits calculation, increasing your benefit amount. If you filed right away, because of the one week lag (your base period ends one week before you file), that last week wouldn't be included.

Maximum and Minimum Limits on Weekly Benefit Amounts

All states have a maximum and minimum limit on the amount of your weekly benefits. Even if you made more than $70,000 during your base period, you wouldn't see a check greater than $175 per week in Arizona if you filed right now. Washington, D.C., and Massachusetts have the highest maximum amount of benefits (anywhere from $335 to $444 per week, the higher amount if you have dependents) while Indiana pays one of the lowest maximum amounts ($116 per week). On the other hand, Hawaii has one of the lowest minimum weekly benefit amounts—$5.00 a week—and New Jersey has one of the highest minimums—$66.00 a week. No matter how much or little you earned during your base period, your state can't pay you more or less than those limits. Those limits are adjusted annually or semiannually in over half the states, so the maximum and minimum limits listed in the chart on pages 49-66 may have changed.

All states pay benefits on the basis of weeks, except New York, which pays on the basis of effective days of unemployment. Weeks usually run from Sunday to Saturday, though some states begin the week on the day you become eligible.

State-by-State Benefits Chart

Now, we can determine whether you qualify to receive benefits and how much those benefits will be. This list includes the 1992 requirements for each state. Some of the figures, like maximum weekly benefit amount, may have changed by now. But the requirements listed here give you a fairly accurate picture as to whether you qualify.

Let's take an example from the chart. Let's say you are unemployed in Idaho. Turn to Idaho in the chart. To qualify for benefits, it says you must have earned at least $1,144 in one quarter during your base period. And you must have made 1.25 times this amount over a two quarter period of time —or $1,430. Your base period is the first four of the last five completed calendar quarters. If you file on June 5, 1993, your base period begins January 1992 and runs to December 31, 1992. During that time, you must have made $1,430. Your base wage method is your highest quarter of earnings. Let's say you made $3,000 during your highest quarter. Now divide your base wage by twenty-six, which is $115. This is your weekly benefit amount.

1.Alabama:

Qualifying wage/hour: You must have wages in at least two quarters of your base period. In your highest quarter of earnings, you must have earned at least $516.01. And your total wages for your base period must be at least 1.5 times your highest quarter earnings.

Weekly benefit amount: (A variation of highest quarter of earnings method.) Divide by twenty-four the average of your two highest quarters.

Min/Max weekly benefit amount: $22-$150.

Base Period: First four of the last five completed calendar quarters preceding the date you file your claim.

2. Alaska:

Qualifying wage/hour: You must have wages of at least $1,000 in two quarters of your base period.

Weekly benefit amount: (Total wages method.) If you are paid less than 90 percent of your wages in one quarter (meaning your wages are spread out over several quarters), you will use all wages paid in the base period to figure out your weekly benefit amount. Multiply your total base wages by .0095. If you were paid 90 percent or more of your wages in one quarter, that quarter won't be used to calculate your weekly benefit amount. Instead, take the total of the other three quarters and multiply that number by ten, then multiply the product by .0095.

Min/Max weekly benefit amount: $44-$212; An additional $24 per dependent is paid up to three dependents.

Base Period: First four of the last five completed calendar quarters preceding the date you file your claim.

3. Arizona:

Qualifying wage/hour: You must have made at least $1,000 during one of your quarters. Your total base period wages must be at least 1.5 times your highest quarter. If you can't make this requirement, your state also provides an alternative calculation: you must have earned wages in two quarters. You must have earned wages in one quarter sufficient to qualify for the maximum weekly benefit amount ($4,362). And you must have earned total base period wages of at least $7,000.

Weekly benefit amount: (Highest Quarter of Earnings Method.) Divide by twenty-five the amount you earned in your highest quarter.

Min/Max weekly benefit amount: $40-$175.

Base Period: First four of the last five completed calendar quarters preceding the date you file your claim.

4. Arkansas:

Qualifying wage/hour: You must have earned twenty-seven times your weekly benefit amount over a two-quarter period. You must have made at least $1,107 during base period and $553 in your highest quarter.

Weekly benefit amount: (Highest Quarter of Earnings Method.) Divide by twenty-six your highest base period quarter.

Min/Max weekly benefit amount: $41-$230.

Base Period: First four of last five completed calendar quarters preceding the date that you filed your claim.

5. California:

Qualifying wage/hour: You must have earned at least $900 in your highest quarter with your total base period wages equal to 1.25 times your highest quarter earnings. Or you must have made $1,300 in your highest quarter.

Weekly Benefit Amount: (Highest Quarter of Earnings Method.) 1/23-1/33 of your highest quarter of earnings.

Min/Max weekly benefit amount: $40-$230.

Base Period: The four quarters ending in June, September, December, or March, depending on the month in which you file your claim.

6. Colorado:

Qualifying wage/hour: You must have made forty times your weekly benefit amount during your base period.

Weekly benefit amount: (Variation on Highest Quarter of Earnings Method.) Your base wage is your two highest quarters. Divide that by twenty-six. Now multiply by 0.55.

Min/Max weekly benefit amount: $25-$239.

Base Period: First four of last five completed calendar quarters preceding the date you filed your claim.

7. Connecticut:

Qualifying wage/hour: You must have earned at least forty times your weekly benefit amount during a two-quarter period. You must have made at least $600 during your base period.

Weekly benefit amount: (Highest Quarter of Earnings Method.) Divide by twenty-six your highest quarter of wages. You may be able to receive dependent's allowance as well.

Min/Max weekly benefit amount: $15-$288; with dependent's allowance: $22-$338.

Base Period: First four of last five completed calendar quarters preceding the date your claim is filed.

8. Delaware:

Qualifying wage/hour: You must have made at least thirty-six times your weekly benefit amount during a two-quarter period. You must have earned at least $965.99 during your highest quarter. If you don't make this requirement, your state allows you to receive reduced benefits if you made at least $720.

Weekly benefit amount: (Variation of Highest Quarter of Earnings Method.) Divide by forty-six the total of your two highest quarters of highest earnings during your base period.

Min/Max weekly benefit amount: $20-$245.

Base Period: First four of the last five completed calendar quarters preceding the date when you filed your claim.

9. District of Columbia:

Qualifying wage/hour: You must have at least $300 in one quarter of your base period. You also must make 1.5 times your highest quarter wages over two quarters. If you fall short by not more than $70, you can still qualify for a reduced benefit amount.

Weekly benefit amount: (Highest Quarter of Earnings Method.) Divide by twenty-three the highest amount of wages earned in a quarter. You may be able to receive dependent's allowance as well.

Min/Max of weekly benefit amount: $13-$335.

Base Period: First four of the last five completed calendar quarters preceding the date when you filed your claim.

10. Florida:

Qualifying wage/hour: You must have worked at least twenty weeks over two quarters and earned at least $20 a week. If you make less than that in a week, that week won't count.

Weekly benefit amount: (Average Weekly Wage Method.) Take 50 percent of your average weekly wage. You find your average weekly wage by dividing your total base period wages by the number of weeks you worked at a job covered by the system.

Min/Max weekly benefit: $10-$225.

Base Period: First four of the last five completed calendar quarters preceding the date when you filed your claim.

11. Georgia:

Qualifying wage/hour: You must have earned 1.5 times your highest quarter of wages over a two-quarter period of time. During your highest quarter you must have made at least $900 and during the base period, you must have made $1,350. If you can't make this qualification, your state provides another: forty times your weekly benefit amount during two quarters.

Weekly benefit amount: (Variation of Highest Quarter of Earnings Method.) Your base wages are your two highest quarters of earnings. Divide your base wage by fifty. If you use the alternative formula, divide your highest quarter of wages by twenty-five.

Min/Max weekly benefit amount: $37-$187.

Base period: First four of the last five completed calendar quarters preceding the date that you file your claim.

12. Hawaii:

Qualifying wage/hour: You must have made twenty-six times your weekly benefit amount over two quarters. During your base period, you must have made at least $130.

Weekly benefit amount: (Highest Quarter of Earnings Method.) Divide by twenty-one the amount you earned in your highest quarter of earnings.

Min/Max weekly benefit amount: $5-$306 weekly benefit amount.

Base Period: First four of the last five completed calendar quarters preceding the date that you file your claim.

13. Idaho:

Qualifying wage/hour: You must be paid at least $1,144 in one quarter during your base period. You must have made 1.25 times your highest quarter of wages over a two-quarter period of time. During the base period, you must have made $1,430.

Weekly benefit amount: (Highest Quarter of Earnings Method.) Divide by twenty-six the amount that you earned in your highest quarter of earnings during your base period.

Min/Max weekly benefit amount: $44-$215.

Base Period: First four of the last five completed calendar quarters preceding the date that you filed your claim.

14. Illinois:

Qualifying wage/hour: You must have earned $1,600 during your base period and at least $440 of that in a quarter outside of your highest quarter of earnings.

Weekly benefit amount: (Variation of Highest Quarter of Earnings Method.) Your base wage is your two highest quarters. Divide your base wage by twenty-six and then multiply by 0.49.

Min/Max weekly benefit amount: $51-$214. With dependent's allowance, your benefits can go as high as $279 a week.

Base Period: First four of the last five completed calendar quarters preceding the date that you file for your benefits.

15. Indiana:

Qualifying wage/hour: You must be paid at least $2,500 during your base period and at least $1,500 in the last two quarters. You must receive wages of 1.25 times your highest quarter of wages during your base period.

Weekly benefit amount: (Highest Quarter of Earnings Method.) Take 5 percent of your first $1,000 of your highest quarter of wages and 4 percent of the remaining highest quarter of wages.

Min/Max weekly benefit amount: $50-$116. Benefit amounts of $134-$171 are available to those with one to three dependents.

Base period: First four of the last five completed calendar quarters preceding the date that you file your claim.

16. Iowa:

Qualifying wage/hour: You must make 1.25 times your highest quarter of wages over two quarters, and also high quarter wages of at least 3.5 percent of the statewide average annual wage. During your high quarter, you must receive at least $670. And over the course of your base period, $1,000.

Weekly benefit amount: (Highest Quarter of Earnings Method.) Divide by twenty-three the amount earned in your highest quarter of the base period. If you have dependents, then you will divide by a lesser number.

Min/Max weekly benefit amount: $29-$194. With dependents: $35-$238.

Base Period: The first four of the last five completed calendar quarters preceding the date your claim is filed.

17. Kansas:

Qualifying wage/hour: You must make at least thirty times your weekly benefit amount during two quarters. And you must receive at least $1,710 during that year.

Weekly benefit amount: (Highest Quarter of Earnings Method.) Multiply your highest quarter of earnings by .0425.

Min/Max weekly benefit amount: $57-$231.

Base period: First four of the last five completed calendar quarters preceding the date when you filed your claim.

18. Kentucky:

Qualifying wage/hour: You must have wages of at least $750 in one quarter and total wages of at least 1.5 times your highest quarter of wages. Also, those wages must be distributed like this: eight times your weekly benefit amount must have been earned in the last two quarters and $750 must have been earned outside your highest quarter.

Weekly benefit amount: (Total Wages Method.) Multiply your total base period wages by .01185.

Min/Max weekly benefit amount: $22-$209.

Base period: First four of the last five calendar quarters preceding the date when you filed your claim.

19. Louisiana:

Qualifying wage/hour: You must make at least $800 in one quarter. You must receive 1.5 times your highest quarter of wages during two quarters. During the base period, you must receive $1,200.

Weekly benefit amount: (Variation on Highest Quarter of Earnings Method.) Add together your four quarters of earnings. Now divide by four. This is your average quarter of earnings. Now divide this by twenty-five. This number should be roughly equal to one-half the amount you earned in a week.

Min/Max weekly benefit amount: $10-$181.

Base Period: First four of the last five completed calendar quarters preceding the date you filed your claim.

20. Maine:

Qualifying wage/hour: You must be paid at least two times the annual average weekly wage in each of two quarters and you must make a total of $2,286.90 during your base period. You also must earn six times the average weekly wage in your base period if you are at the maximum weekly benefit amount level.

Weekly benefit amount: (Highest Quarter of Earnings Method.) Divide by twenty-two your highest quarter of wages, not including allowance for dependents.

Min/Max weekly benefit amount: $35-$198; with dependents: $52-$297.

Base period: First four of the last five completed calendar quarters preceding the date you file your claim.

21. Maryland:

Qualifying wage/hour: You must have received at least $576.01 in one quarter, and you must earn during your base period 1.5 times the upper limit of the highest quarterly earnings shown on a schedule provided by your unemployment office. You must have wages for two quarters of your base period. If you don't make this, your state provides you a lesser amount of benefits.

Weekly benefit amount: (Highest Quarter of Earnings Method.) Divide by twenty-four your highest quarter of wages. You may also be eligible for dependent allowance.

Min/Max weekly benefit amount: $25-$223.

Base Period: First four of the last five completed calendar quarters preceding the date when you first file your claim.

22. Massachusetts:

Qualifying wage/hour: You must earn at least thirty times your weekly benefit amount. You must have been earned at least $1,800 during your base year.

Weekly benefit amount: (Highest Quarter of Earnings Method.) Divide by twenty-one your highest quarter of wages.

Min/Max weekly benefit amount: $14-$296; with dependent's allowance: $21-$444.

Base Period: Use the fifty-two consecutive calendar weeks immediately prior to filing your claim.

23. Michigan:

Qualifying wage/hour: You must have worked at least twenty weeks and you must have earned thirty times the state's minimum hourly wage ($3.35 as of 1/23/92). During your base period you must have made at least $2,010. If you don't qualify under this formula, your state provides another one: you must have worked fourteen weeks and your base period wages must be equal to twenty times your state's average weekly wage ($489.01 as of 1/23/92).

Weekly benefit amount: (An "After-Tax Version of Average Weekly Wage Method.) Your base wage is your average after tax weekly wage earned during your base period. Multiply that by .70.

Min/Max weekly benefit amount: $60-$283.

Base Period: Take the fifty-two consecutive calendar weeks immediately prior to filing your claim.

24. Minnesota:

Qualifying wage/hour: You must have worked at least fifteen weeks during your base period. During one quarter, you must have received at least $1,000. And you must be paid at least 1.25 times your highest quarter of wages over a two-quarter period.

Weekly benefit amount: (Highest Quarter of Earnings Method.) Divide by twenty-six your highest quarter of wages. Min/Max weekly benefit amount: $38-$265.

Base Period: First four of the last five completed calendar quarters preceding the date when you filed your claim.

25. Mississippi:

Qualifying wage/hour: You must have earned forty times your weekly benefit amount during your base period over two quarters.Your highest quarter of wages can't be less than twenty-six times the minimum weekly benefit amount. Your highest quarter must not be less than $780 and you must have earned $1,200 during your base year.

Weekly benefit amount: (Highest Quarter of Earnings Method.) Divide by twenty-six your highest quarter of wages. Min/Max weekly benefit amount: $30-$165.

Base Period: First four of the last five completed calendar quarters preceding the date that you file for benefits.

26. Missouri:

Qualifying wage/hour: During one quarter, you must make at least $1,000. And you must have received 1.5 times your highest quarter of wages during your base year over two quarters. If this doesn't work for you, your state provides another way to qualify: your wages in two quarters must be 1.5 times the maximum taxable wage base for that year.

Weekly benefit amount: (Highest Quarter of Earnings Method.) Multiply your highest quarter of wages by .045.

Min/Max weekly benefit amount: $45-$175.

Base Period: First four of the last five completed calendar quarters preceding the date when you filed for benefits.

27.Montana:

Qualifying wage/hour: You must have received 1.5 times your highest quarter of wages during your base period over two quarters. During your base period, you must make a total of $5,000. Your total base period wages must equal at least 7 percent of the average annual wage.

Weekly benefit amount: (Total Wage Method.) Your base wage is your total annual wage in your base period. Multiply that by .01. Or your base wage can be your two highest quarters of earnings. Then multiply that by .019.

Min/Max weekly benefit amount:$50-$201.

Base Period: First four of the last five completed calendar quarters preceding the date when you filed for benefits.

28. Nebraska:

Qualifying wage/hour: You must make $1,200 during your base period, and in each of two quarters, you must make $400 in wages.

Weekly benefit amount: (Scaled Version of Highest Quarter of Earnings Method.) 1/20-1/24 of your highest quarter of earnings. Min/Max weekly benefit amount: $20-$154.

Base Period: Take the first four completed calendar quarters preceding the date when you filed for benefits. Your legislature may have changed it, however, to the first four of the last five completed calendar quarters.

29. Nevada:

Qualifying wage/hour: You must make 1.5 times your highest quarter of wages over two quarters. You must earn at least $400 during your highest quarter. If this doesn't work for you, you can also qualify by earning wages in three of the four quarters in the base period.

Weekly benefit amount: (Highest Quarter of Earnings Method.) Divide by twenty-five your highest quarter of earnings.

Min/Max weekly benefit amount: $16-$211.

Base Period: Take the first four of the last five completed calendar quarters preceding the date when you filed for benefits.

30. New Hampshire:

Qualifying wage/hour: You must earn $2,800 during your base period and at least $1,200 in each of two quarters.

Weekly benefit amount: (Total Wage Method.) Your base wage is your annual wage during your base period. Multiply your base wage by 0.008 up to 0.014. Use the higher percentage if you didn't make a lot of money.

Min/Max weekly benefit amount: $32-$188.

Base Period: The calendar year starting April 1st to March 31.

31. New Jersey:

Qualifying wage/hour: You must work twenty weeks and make at least 20 percent of the statewide average weekly wage (now at $110) for each of those weeks. If you don't make that much, the week doesn't count. During your base period, you must have earned at least $2,200. Another way to qualify is this: you must have made twelve times your state's average weekly wage—about $6,600—in your base period. If you're an agricultural worker, you must have worked 770 hours.

Weekly benefit amount: (Average Weekly Wage Method.) Multiply your average weekly wage by 0.60. If applicable, you can collect dependent's allowance as well. To calculate your average wage, take your total wages during your base period and divide that by the number of weeks that you worked.

Min/Max weekly benefit amount: $66-$308.

Base Period: First four of the last five completed calendar quarters preceding the date when you filed your first claim.

32. New Mexico:

Qualifying wage/hour: Your total base period wages must be at least 1.25 times your highest quarter of wages. And those wages must be spread out over at least two quarters. During one quarter, you must make at least $963 and during your base period, you must make at a minimum $1,204.

Weekly benefit amount: (Highest Quarter of Earnings Method.) Take your highest quarter of wages during your base period and divide by twenty-six.

Min/Max weekly benefit amount: $37-$185.

Base Period: First four of the last five completed calendar quarters preceding the date when you filed your first claim.

33. New York:

Qualifying wage/hour: You must work at least twenty weeks during your base period with your minimum average weekly wage equal to at least $80 a week. During your base period, you must make at least $1,600. If this formula doesn't work, your state also provides another: You worked fifteen weeks and you earned at least the minimum weekly wage a week and you must have a total of forty weeks over two years preceding your base year and you earned at least the minimum wage during those forty weeks.

Weekly benefit amount: (Average Weekly Wage Method.) Take 50 percent of your average weekly wage. To calculate your average weekly wage take the total of your base period wages divided by the number of weeks of employment. Don't count weeks where you made less than $80.

Min/Max weekly benefit amount: $40-$300.

Base Period: There's a one week lag between when you file a valid claim and when your base period ends.

34. North Carolina:

Qualifying wage/hour: You must make 1.5 times your highest quarter of wages over a two quarter period of time. During at least one quarter, you must make at least $581 and during your base period, at least $2,323. If you are at the maximum weekly benefit amount, you must also earn six times your state's average weekly wage.

Weekly benefit amount: (Variation of Highest Quarter of Earnings Method.) Divide by fifty-two your two highest quarters of your earnings.

Min/Max weekly benefit amount: $22-$258.

Base Period: First four of the last five completed calendar quarters preceding the date when you filed your first claim.

35. North Dakota:

Qualifying wage/hour: You must make 1.3 times your highest quarter of wages over two quarters. During one quarter, you must make at least $1,118 and during the base period, you must make at a minimum $2,795.

Weekly benefit amount: (Variation of Highest Quarter of Earnings Method.) Divide by sixty-five your total wages earned in your two highest earning quarters. Then divide by two your total wages in the third quarter and add this to your amount.

Min/Max weekly benefit amount: $43-$206.

Base Period: First four of the last five completed calendar quarters preceding the date when you filed your first claim.

36. Ohio:

Qualifying wage/hour: You must work at least twenty weeks during your base period and earn an average weekly wage equaling 27.5 percent of the state average weekly wage. During your base period, you must earn at least $1,702.

Weekly benefit amount: (Average Weekly Wage Method.) Multiply your average weekly wage by 0.50. Your average weekly wage is your total earnings in all the weeks you earned more than $20 divided by that number of weeks. You may also qualify for dependent's allowance.

Min/Max weekly benefit amount: $42-$211. With dependent's allowance, $294. Your average weekly wage is the total of your earnings divided by the weeks in which you earned at least $20.

Base Period: First four of the last five completed calendar quarters preceding the date when you filed your first claim.

37. Oklahoma:

Qualifying wage/hour: You need to make 40 percent of taxable wage base. And your total base period wages must be at least 1.5 times your highest quarter of wages over a two quarter period. During your highest quarter, you must earn a minimum of $2,693. Another way to qualify is the following: earn $10,100 during your base period.

Weekly benefit amount: (Highest Quarter of Earnings Method.) Divide by twenty-five your highest quarter of earnings.

Min/Max weekly benefit amount: $16-$212.

Base Period: First four of the last five completed calendar quarters preceding the date when you filed your first claim.

38. Oregon:

Qualifying wage/hour: You must have worked at least eighteen weeks and made at least $1,000 during your base period. Your state does not specify a weekly amount that you must earn. That $1,000 must be spread out over two quarters.

Weekly benefit amount: (Total Wage Method.) Your base wage is your total wage. Multiply your base wage by 0.0125.

Min/Max weekly benefit amount: $60-$239.

Base Period: First four of the last five completed calendar quarters preceding the date when you filed your first claim.

39. Pennsylvania:

Qualifying wage/hour: You must have worked at least sixteen weeks at a weekly minimum amount of $50. And you must earn at least forty times your weekly benefit amount during the benefit year and one-fifth of those wages must be made outside your highest quarter. If you don't make these requirements, you may be able to receive reduced benefits anyway.

Weekly benefit amount: (Highest Quarter of Earnings Method.) Divide by twenty-three or twenty-five your highest quarter of earnings. Or take 50 percent of your full time weekly wage, if this amount is greater.

Min/Max weekly benefit amount: $35-$304. With dependence: $40-$312.

Base Period: First four of the last five completed calendar quarters preceding the date when you filed your first claim.

40. Puerto Rico:

Qualifying wage/hour: You must earn wages in at least two quarters of your base period. And during your base period, you must have earned at least $280. And you must earn forty times your weekly benefit amount. If you're an agricultural worker, you may qualify on the basis of earnings in a single quarter. During your high quarter, you must make at least $75 and during the base period, you must make $280. Even if you don't make these requirements, you may be able to receive some benefits.

Weekly benefit amount: (Scaled Version of Highest Quarter of Earnings Method.) Divide by eleven and up to twenty-six your highest quarter of earnings.

Min/Max weekly benefit amount: $7-$120. If you work in agriculture, then your range is $10-$40.

Base Period: First four of the last five completed calendar quarters preceding the date when you filed your first claim.

41. Rhode Island:

Qualifying wage/hour: You must make 200 times the minimum hourly wage in one quarter and total base period wages of 1.5 times your highest quarter of wages. The base period wages must be at least 400 times the minimum hourly wage. During your highest quarter, you must make $890. Your state provides another way to qualify: earn 12,000 times the total minimum hourly wage in your base period.

Weekly benefit amount: (Highest Quarter of Earnings Method.) Multiply your highest quarter of earnings by 0.0462.

Min/Max weekly benefit amount: $41-$285; with dependent's allowance: $51-$365.

Base Period: First four of the last five completed calendar quarters preceding the date when you filed your first claim.

42. South Carolina:

Qualifying wage/hour: You must be paid at least $540 in a quarter during your base period. Also you must make 1.5 times your highest quarterly wage over a two quarter period. And at least $900 during your base year.

Weekly benefit amount: (Variation of Highest Quarter of Earnings Method.) Take 50 percent of your average weekly wage during your highest quarter. Your average weekly wage is found by dividing your total wages in your high quarter by thirteen.

Min/Max weekly benefit amount: $20-$186.

Base Period: First four of the last five completed calendar quarters preceding the date when you filed your first claim.

43. South Dakota:

Qualifying wage/hour: You must have received wages in at least two quarters during your base period. And you must earn a minimum of $728 during your highest quarter of wages and the total of the other three quarters must amount to at least thirty times your weekly benefit amount.

Weekly benefit amount: (Highest Quarter of Earnings Method.) Divide by twenty-six your highest quarter of earnings.

Min/Max weekly benefit amount: $28-$154.

Base Period: First four of the last five completed calendar quarters preceding the date when you filed your first claim.

44. Tennessee:

Qualifying wage/hour: You must make forty times your weekly benefit amount over two quarters. During your highest quarter you must make a minimum of $780.

Weekly benefit amount: (Variation of Highest Quarter of Earnings Method.) Take your two highest quarters and divide by two. This is your average high quarter earnings. Now divide by twenty-six or thirty-two, the higher number if you made a lot of money.

Min/Max weekly benefit amount: $30-$170.

Base Period: First four of the last five completed calendar quarters preceding the date when you filed your first claim.

45. Texas:

Qualifying wage/hour: You must earn thirty-seven times your weekly benefit amount over a two quarter period. And during your base period, you must earn a minimum of $1,406.

Weekly benefit amount: (Highest Quarter of Earnings Method.) Divide by twenty-five your highest quarter of earnings.

Min/max weekly benefit amount: $38-$231.

Base Period: First four of the last five completed calendar quarters preceding the date when you filed your first claim.

46. Utah:

Qualifying wage/hour: You must earn at least $375 during one quarter of your base period. In your base period, you must make 1.5 times your highest quarter of wages. Another way to qualify: You must have twenty weeks of work and 8 percent of the state's average year of wages.

Weekly benefit amount: (Highest Quarter of Earnings Method.) Divide by twenty-six your highest quarter of wages in your base year.

Min/Max weekly benefit amount: $14-$230.

Base period: First four of the last five completed calendar quarters preceding the date when you filed your first claim.

47. Vermont:

Qualifying wage/hours You must earn at least $1,054 during your highest quarter and base period wages of at least 40 percent of the total highest quarter wages.

Weekly benefit amount: (Variation of Highest Quarter of Earnings Method.) Divide the wages from your two highest quarters by forty-five.

Min/Max weekly benefit amount: $26-$192.

Base Period: First four of the last five completed calendar quarters preceding the date when you filed your first claim. If you don't meet the qualifying wage for this period, your office may make a determination based on another base period—so apply anyway.

48. Virginia:

Qualifying wage/hour: You must earn fifty times your weekly benefit amount during a two-quarter period. Your minimum earnings during your highest quarter must be $1,625. And you must earn at least $3,250 during your base period.

Weekly benefit amount: (Variation of Highest Quarter of Earnings Method.) Divide by fifty your two highest quarters of earnings.

Min/Max weekly benefit amount: $65-$208.

Base Period: First four of the last five completed calendar quarters preceding the date when you filed your first claim.

49. Virgin Islands:

Qualifying wage/hour: During one quarter, you must earn at least $858. And you must earn 1.5 times your highest quarter of wages over two quarters. If this doesn't help you to qualify, try this alternative formula: Earn $858 in your highest quarter and thirty-nine times your weekly benefit amount during your base period.

Weekly benefit amount: (Highest Quarter of Earnings Method.) Divide by twenty-six your highest quarter of earnings.

Min/Max weekly benefit amount: $32-$191.

Base Period: First four of the last five completed calendar quarters preceding the date when you filed your first claim.

50. Washington:

Qualifying wage/hour: You must work 680 hours during your base period.

Weekly benefit amount: (Highest Quarter of Earnings Method.) Add together your two highest quarters. Then divide this by two. This is your average highest quarter of earnings. Now divide this by twenty-five.

Min/Max weekly benefit amount: $64-$258.

Base Period: First four of the last five completed calendar quarters preceding the date when you filed your first claim.

51. West Virginia:

Qualifying wage/hour: You must earn at least $2,200 during your base period over a two quarter period of time.

Weekly benefit amount: (Total Wage Method.) Multiply your total wage by 0.01.

Min/Max weekly benefit amount: $24-$263.

Base Period: First four of the last five completed calendar quarters preceding the date when you filed your first claim.

52. Wisconsin:

Qualifying wage/hour: During one quarter, you must earn at least $1,075. You must make in total wages at least thirty times your weekly benefit amount. Eight times your weekly benefit amount must be earned outside the highest quarter and these earnings must be spread out over two quarters.

Weekly benefit amount: (Highest Quarter of Earnings Method.) Multiply your highest quarter of earnings by 0.04.

Min/Max weekly benefit amount: $43-$230.

Base Period: First four of the last five completed calendar quarters preceding the date when you filed your first claim.

53. Wyoming:

Qualifying wage/hour: You must be paid for at least two quarters. And during one quarter, you must make at least $1.000 (5 percent of the state-wide average annual wage). You must earn at a minimum 1.6 times your highest quarter of wages over two quarters. Total base period wages must be at least 8 percent of your state average annual wage (around $1,600).

Weekly benefit amount: (Highest Quarter of Earnings Method.) Multiply your highest quarter of earnings by 0.04.

Min/Max weekly benefit amount: $38-$200.

Base Period: First four of the last five completed calendar quarters preceding the date when you filed your first claim.

Source: U.S. Department of Labor: Employment and Training Administration, Unemployment Insurance Service: Comparison of State Unemployment Insurance Laws, January, 1992.

Waiting Period

After you file for benefits, almost every state requires that you be partially or totally unemployed for one week. This is called the *waiting week*. During that week, you will not receive any benefits. The waiting period is considered the first week in your benefit year—the fifty-two week period that you have to collect your twenty-six weeks worth of checks. After the week goes by, you start receiving benefits.

All states except the following have a waiting period: Alabama, Connecticut, Delaware, Georgia, Iowa, Kentucky, Maryland, Michigan, Nevada, New Hampshire, and Wisconsin. In some states, you are compensated for the waiting week: Missouri, New Jersey, Texas, and Minnesota.

The waiting period requirement also applies if you are partially unemployed; that is, if you are trying to collect benefits because you are partially unemployed, you must be fully unemployed for one full week. But there are exceptions. In Alabama, you can be partially unemployed during that one week before your benefits are paid to you. In New York, the four "effective days" which make up the waiting period may be accumulated in one, two, three, or four weeks. In Montana, no waiting period is required for benefits if you are partially unemployed.

Fraud

Some people work without reporting it to the unemployment office. Not only will you have to repay your benefits, but you could be criminally charged with fraud, and have to pay fines or jail time.

How Long You Can Collect Your Benefits

In most states, you receive twenty-six weeks worth of benefits. You have a certain amount of time to collect these benefits and then the funnel is turned off—Zap! You've got to get another job, get laid off, or voluntarily quit for a good reason and repeat the process.

Extensions

Times are tough. Jobs are scarce. The country's unemployment rate is steadily going up like a temperature gauge on a hot summer day. During economic recessions and especially right before presidential elections, the federal government often passes legislation so that you can receive your weekly benefits for longer than twenty-six weeks. These benefits are paid to you at the same rate as your weekly benefit amount. The government realizes that when the economy is slow, it's more difficult to find a job, so they give you more time to collect benefits while you look. Even if the unemployment rate is low for the country, certain states with high unemployment may pass a law extending its benefit payments. Generally, if your state pays weekly benefits for twenty-six weeks, an additional thirteen weeks of benefits are added on top of that.

If you have job skills in an outdated area of employment, you may be able to receive an extension as you become trained in another area. Be sure to check with the unemployment office about this because there are time limits for when you can apply for this type of extension.

Special Circumstances: Part-Time Work

Carol tacks up fliers offering to tutor students in Italian. She receives some calls and is interested in providing this service, but wonders if she'll lose her benefits if she earns a little income this way.

In almost all states she can still receive benefits, as long as she is earning less than her weekly benefit amount. You will receive partial benefits in this case—the difference between your weekly benefit amount and wages earned. Some states let you keep some of your wages from part-time work. For example, in states where wages in excess of $5 are considered, if you earn only $5 in partial employment, you would receive the full benefit amount. If your weekly benefit check was $26 and you earned $10 for the week, you would receive $21, $26 less $5 (wages in excess of $5). Your benefits plus wages would amount to $31 or $5 more than your weekly benefit check.

Other states allow you to earn a certain percentage of your weekly benefit amount in part-time work without losing your benefits. In Louisiana, you can earn one-half of your weekly benefits; in the District of Columbia, two-fifths, in Oregon, one-third, in Colorado, one-fourth, and in New Mexico, one-fifth.

Michigan and Wisconsin will pay you your full weekly benefits if your earnings are less than half of your weekly benefits, but if your wages are one-half or more, you only receive half of your weekly benefit amount.

North Carolina, however, only allows you to work two full-time days. If you go over that, you are no longer considered unemployed. In Puerto Rico, you are considered unemployed and therefore eligible for benefits as long as your wages and money from odd jobs amount to less than two times the weekly benefit amount.

If you are eligible for partial benefits, you may also receive extra money for dependents which is called "dependent's allowance."

Dependent's Allowance

If you financially support your children or are married, many states pay an additional benefit amount—usually a fixed amount—for dependents. A dependent must be wholly or mainly supported by you, or living with, or receiving regular support from you. All states limit the number of dependents that you can claim, with few allowing for four or more.

Thirteen states and the District of Columbia pay dependent's allowance: Alaska, Connecticut, Washington, D.C., Illinois, Indiana, Iowa, Maine, Maryland, Massachusetts, Michigan, New Jersey, Ohio, Pennsylvania, and Rhode Island.

Some states include dependents other than children. Nonworking spouses (Connecticut); your unemployed spouse (New Jersey); a legally married spouse living with and being wholly or partially supported by you (Iowa and Pennsylvania); spouses with a disability and unable to work (D.C.); and dependent parents, brothers, or sisters who are unable to work because of age or disability (Iowa, Washington, D.C., Michigan).

Training Courses

If you are in a retraining course to increase your employment opportunities, you may be able to receive benefits for a longer period of time. In Massachusetts and Michigan, you can receive an amount equal to eighteen times the weekly benefit amount while attending a course approved by the unemployment agency. California pays benefits under the state extended benefits program during retraining. In New York, you can receive additional benefits up to 104 effective days. Ask at your unemployment office for a list of approved courses.

Seasonal Work

If you work primarily in seasonal employment, you face an uphill battle collecting benefits. In most states, no distinction is made between wages received from a seasonal employer and a regular employer. Your right to benefits are determined under the same benefit provisions. For example, a professional baseball player was employed on an annual basis for an annual salary, even though his salary was paid in five monthly installments during the regular season. Just because he wasn't required to play ball during the off-season didn't alter his employment status, because he was required to present himself as ready to play and was paid to do so.

The problem here is that you might not have earned enough wages or worked long enough to qualify. Or, if you do qualify, you may quickly be disqualified when there is no suitable work available for your skills until the next season rolls around. If you are willing to work other kinds of jobs, then you will have less problems proving your availability.

Moving: Interstate and In-State Claims

If you are laid off in one state and qualify for benefits there, you can move to another state and still receive those benefits. Your original state will send you checks.

At her job designing clothes, Dale put in an application to be transferred from Spokane to Seattle, Washington. Her company approved the transfer. After three months working in Seattle, her company laid her off because business slowed.

Dale filed for benefits based on her job as a clothes designer. She will be eligible to collect benefits in Seattle using a base period that covers her earnings in Spokane and Seattle.

Workshare Programs

Business is slow. Your employer decides that instead of laying off employees, she will reduce hours. Your work week is cut back by fifteen hours. Can you collect unemployment benefits?

Check and see if your employer entered a worksharing plan with a union and received final approval by the state employment security agency. If so, you may be able to receive partial benefits, even though you are not actively seeking a new job, nor available for other work. States that allow workshare plans include: Arizona, Arkansas, California, Florida, Iowa, Kansas, Louisiana, Maryland, Massachusetts, Missouri, New York, Oregon, Rhode Island, Texas, Vermont, and Washington.

Disability Benefits

In five states and one dependency (California, New Jersey, Rhode Island, New York, Hawaii and Puerto Rico) you can receive disability benefits if you become ill or disabled when you are not at work, whether you are employed or unemployed at the time. Ask about disability benefits at the unemployment office. They can tell you where and how to file.

Creditors

In most instances, a creditor (someone to whom you owe money) can't take your benefits as long as you keep your payments in a separate bank account from the other money you have.

Chapter 4

Filing Your Claim

Thursday, 9:35 A.M. Standing in line reading his magazine, Jose Medina mumbles to himself that he should have arrived at the unemployment office earlier. A fog hangs outside the office door, where the long line of people will soon join it. Jose, number 168 in line, was recently laid off from his job selling furniture. He's hoping to receive at least $300 a month to help pay the rent. Every few minutes, he glances up to the black-and-white industrial clock in the office. It now reads 10:00 A.M. Behind him, another fifty unemployed people stand and wait, some dressed in suits with neatly combed hair, others in jeans and T-shirts, and some looking like they just rolled out of bed. Twenty minutes later, he's almost at the front of the line, near the window. No one says much, only the shuffle of feet or the turning of a page in a book is heard.

Yesterday, Jose picked up the unemployment benefits form. When he sat down with the forms, he couldn't decide if he should check the box "Laid Off" or "Discharged." So he went ahead and circled the latter.

When Jose finally makes it to the front of the line, the unemployment agent writes down his social security number from his card and looks at his completed form. "Here, on this line, you say that you were laid off because business was slow," said the agent. "Then here, you check off the box, 'discharged.' Which do you mean?"

Flustered, Jose explains that his boss let him go because no one was buying furniture. He didn't do anything wrong. The boss just had to let him go.

"Check 'Laid Off,'" said the agent. Jose doesn't argue and checks the appropriate box. By now, the line has seeped into the fog. At least 300 more to go. Then another couple hundred until the office closes for another day.

Three weeks later Jose receives his money. Yet many people, confused by the unemployment benefits terminology, would not see a check so soon. A major source of delay is checking the wrong box to indicate how you lost your job. If you check the "terminated" box or the "discharged" box, you are telling the unemployment office that your employer fired you because you did something wrong. Now your claim receives a closer inspection by the unemployment office. And, more importantly, you've increased your chance of not receiving any money, at least not right away.

Before you fill out your initial claim form for benefits, read this chapter. You'll find most of your questions answered here or you'll become aware of the right questions to ask the unemployment agent when you turn in your form.

A Quick Overview of the Process

The initial claim form could be your worst nightmare—leading you through a bureaucratic nightmare lasting months upon months, stacks of papers, and difficult people, who act like their main purpose in life is to prevent you from receiving benefits. If you persevere, file the forms, answer questions and more questions, still, after months have passed, you may never see a dime.

Or this claim form could be a beeline to a steady stream of money to tide you over until you find a job. In other words, you are standing at a huge juncture in the road, and the decisions you make now take on great importance because of the wildly different scenarios that could follow.

To help you make the right decisions, sample initial claim forms are included here for the state of California, although most states' forms will look similar and ask similar questions. The forms are designed to elicit information regarding your work history and to determine your eligibility to receive benefits.

As you glance over the paperwork, you will see that it provides very little room for long explanations. For example, when you are asked why you no longer work at your last job, you are given several dotted lines for your explanation. This is a not-so-subtle hint that your response should be simple and concise. Now is not the time for a treatise on how lousy your boss treated you or the unsanitary condition of your workplace. Nor is it a time to sell yourself, explaining what a great worker you are, that anyone would be glad to hire you. Just give the facts.

After the unemployment office receives your application, a form is sent to your former employer to let her know that you are applying for benefits and to provide an opportunity for your employer to respond if she has facts relating to your eligibility. Typically, most states give the employer ten days to challenge an employee's application for benefits. If, after that time, the employer wants to respond, she must provide a good reason why she didn't make the deadline. Both you and your former employer, if she responds, will be interviewed either in person or over the phone about your claim for benefits. Even if your employer does not respond, the unemployment agent will make a determination based on the information that you provided on the form and in the interview.

Check List for Filing For Unemployment Benefits

❑ Don't wait to file your claim form. Although you might not need the money right away, it takes time for the unemployment office to process your form and for you to receive your benefits. And if you now live in a different state and are filing for benefits from your old state, it will take even longer to receive any money. As you've read in chapter three on benefits, the way your benefits are calculated depends on when you file. If you wait too long, part of your unemployment time might be included in the formula, reducing your benefit amount.

❑ Bring your social security card. If you've lost it, call the Social Security office and get a new card. If you have an identification card that includes your social security number, some unemployment offices may accept this.

❑ Bring something to read in case there is a long line. Mondays and the day after holidays tend to be the busiest and the longest wait. If long lines drive you crazy, try a Tuesday or Wednesday, instead. Most often, the states' unemployment benefits offices open at 8:00 A.M. You'll have less of a wait if you show up early.

❑ If you are an alien, bring your alien registration card or other documents issued by the Immigration and Naturalization Service or any documents that show your immigration status.

❑ Know the name and address of your last employer. If you can, also write down the name and addresses of all employers for the last year, including employers in other states. You will need this information to fill out the initial claim form.

❑ Ask an unemployment benefits employee for a "claimant's handbook" for information about specific aspects about the system in your state. This pamphlet may be called something else in your state.

The Initial Claim Form 1—Tips

Tip 1: **Question 9.** Keep your responses simple and concise. Chapter two concerning eligibility discusses the many ways you can leave work and still receive benefits. Here's a quick review:

If you were laid off because business was slow, just write "Laid Off." If you were discharged, but not because of misconduct, write "discharged without any misconduct on my part." If you quit for good reasons connected with work (or personal reasons, depending on your state) write in "quit for good cause work-related reason." Or if you are in a state that allows you to quit for personal reasons write "quit for good cause personal reason." Read the section on "How to Argue Your Appeal" for a voluntary quit in chapter five as a guide to explaining how your reason fits into the unemployment office's definition of a "good cause."

That's it. Don't say anything more. In the interview, you will expand on the particular reason why you are now unemployed. For example, if you voluntarily quit for work reasons, you would say something like the following in your interview, "I had to quit because my workplace conditions threatened my health," assuming this were true. Or you quit because of poor working conditions; too much dust in the

1. SOCIAL SECURITY ACCOUNT NUMBER	2. PRINT YOUR FIRST NAME INITIAL LAST NAME	3. BIRTH DATE	4.
_ _ _ — _ _ — _ _ _ _		_ _ / _ _ / _ _	MALE FEMALE ☐ ☐

5. PRINT ADDRESS AT WHICH YOU RECEIVE YOUR MAIL	APT.	CITY	ZIP CODE

6. **YOUR** PHONE NUMBER	7. PRINT OTHER LAST NAMES AND SSA NOS. YOU HAVE USED IN LAST TWO YEARS.	8. LAST DATE YOU WORKED IN YOUR **LAST** JOB.
( )		_ _ / _ _ / _ _

9. EXPLAIN IN YOUR OWN WORDS THE REASON FOR LEAVING YOUR **LAST** JOB.

A. EFF. DATE OF CLAIM

EMPLOYER OR COMPANY	10. NAME AND MAILING ADDRESS OF YOUR VERY **LAST** EMPLOYER	11. MARK THE APPROPRIATE BLOCK TO INDICATE WHY YOU ARE NO LONGER WORKING ON YOUR **LAST** JOB.	B. OFFICE NO.	C. ☐ NEW ☐ AC ☐ RC
STREET OR BOX NO.		☐ Laid Off Due to Lack of Work (This includes temporary layoff)	D. ☐ UI	E. ☐ UCFE	F. ☐ UCX
CITY AND STATE	_ _ _ — _ _ _ ZIP CODE	☐ Discharged (Fired) ☐ Voluntary Quit ☐ Strike or Lockout	G. ☐ W ☐ S	☐ E ☐ B	H. C.S.
			I. ☐ TRANSI-TIONAL	J. WP PRIOR ☐ 1254

R. FOR DEPARTMENT USE ONLY		☐ Corrected Notice	P. DOT	Q. SIC	CHO	K. H.S.	L. PER FREQ
Date		INTERVIEWER				M.	N. OC	O. SWP

12. In the past 19 months did you:

Serve in the armed forces? . . . . ☐ Yes ☐ No

Work for an agency of the Federal Government? . . . . ☐ Yes ☐ No

Work for an employer in another state? . . . . ☐ Yes ☐ No

13. Have you filed a claim or claimed benefits for unemployment insurance against California, another state, or the Federal Government in the past 12 months? . . . . ☐ Yes ☐ No

14. Have you received or do you expect to receive any payments from your last employer other than your regular salary? . . . . ☐ Yes ☐ No

15. Are you physically able and willing to take a full-time job in your usual occupation? . . . . ☐ Yes ☐ No

16. Is there **any** reason that would interfere with your accepting immediate and **full-time** work? . . . . ☐ Yes ☐ No

17. Are you enrolled in or planning to enroll in a training course or school? . . . . ☐ Yes ☐ No

18. Are you self-employed or do you plan to become self-employed, including farming or ranching? . . . . ☐ Yes ☐ No

19. Are you self-incorporated, an officer or major stockholder of a corporation? . . . . ☐ Yes ☐ No

20. Are you a member of a union? (If yes, answer 20A, 20B, and 20C below.) . . . . ☐ Yes ☐ No

20A. Name of union_____ 20B. Union number _____

20C. Are you registered as out of work with your union? . . . . ☐ Yes ☐ No

21. Are you receiving a pension other than Social Security benefits, which is based on **your** prior work? **Examples of pension or retirement payments are military retired pay, union pension, etc.** (If yes, answer 21A and 21B below.) . . . . ☐ Yes ☐ No

21A. Enter the source of pension _____

21B. Enter the gross pension amount you receive before deductions for income tax, health continuation plan, etc., $ _____ per month.

If you begin receiving a pension at a later date, you must report the pension when you receive it. You may be required to repay Unemployment Insurance benefits received for the period covered by a retroactive pension payment.

22. I certify that I am a United States citizen or national . . . . ☐ Yes ☐ No

OR

In a satisfactory immigration status, which I understand to mean a status under which I am residing in the United States lawfully and am legally authorized to work . . . . ☐ Yes ☐ No

23. I was a United States citizen or national for all of the 19 months prior to this filing. If "No" is checked: I was an alien who was lawfully admitted to the United States for permanent residence, lawfully present in the United States for performing services, or permanently residing in the United States under color of law for all of the nineteen months prior to this filing: . . . . ☐ Yes ☐ No

If "No", Reason: _____

I hereby claim benefits and register for work. I am unemployed or working part-time. I have answered these questions knowing that the law provides penalties for making false statements. As to question 22, citizenship status, I declare under penalty of perjury, under the laws of the State of California that my answer is truthful. I understand that the information I provide on this form will be sent to my last employer and may be released to other government agencies to the extent allowed by law.

CLAIMANT — DO NOT SIGN UNTIL ASKED TO DO SO. X _____

You have filed your claim only when this form is reviewed and accepted by the Department.

FOR ISSUE DATE OCT 27 1992

RETURN COMPLETED FORM ON _____ AT _____   A.M. P.M.

TO WINDOW/BASKET/SECTION _____

EDD Serving the People of California

DE 1101B Rev. 11 (4-90) UI CLAIM State of California / Employment Development Department

EDD Serving the People of California

FOR SPECIAL OFFICE USE ONLY
INTAKE FIELD OFFICE NO.
INTAKE STAFF SDC
ACTIVITY DATE

APPLICATION FOR SERVICE

1. SOCIAL SECURITY NUMBER	2. LAST NAME	FIRST	INITIAL

3. DATE OF BIRTH Mo. Day Yr.	4. MALE FEMALE 1 ☐ 2 ☐	5. MAILING ADDRESS — NUMBER AND STREET APT.	CITY	STATE

6. ZIP CODE	7. COUNTY	8. TELEPHONE NUMBER ( )	9. ARE YOU A U.S. CITIZEN OR NATIONAL? ☐ YES ☐ NO

10. LOWEST WAGE YOU WILL ACCEPT TO START A JOB? $ _____ per ☐ HOUR ☐ WEEK ☐ YEAR ☐ DAY ☐ MONTH ☐ OTHER	11. ARE YOU EMPLOYED (INCLUDES TEMPORARY, PART-TIME OR SELF EMPLOYED)? ☐ Yes ☐ No	12. ARE YOU CURRENTLY IN SCHOOL FULL-TIME OR BETWEEN TERMS? ☐ Yes ☐ No

13. ENTER HIGHEST SCHOOL GRADE COMPLETED:	14. COLLEGE DEGREE? (SPECIFY TYPE, E.G., BA) ☐ Yes ☐ No	15. ATTENDED VOCATIONAL TRAINING? ☐ Yes ☐ No IF YES, DESCRIBE THE TRAINING AND CERTIFICATES RECEIVED:

16. DO YOU HAVE A VALID CALIFORNIA DRIVERS LICENSE? ☐ YES ☐ NO	IF YES, WHICH TYPE? ☐ REGULAR CLASS 3 OR C ☐ CLASS 1 OR A ☐ CLASS 2 OR B ☐ CLASS 4 OR M

17. WHAT HOURS, DAYS, SHIFTS, ARE YOU WILLING TO WORK?	18. WILL YOU WORK: ☐ PART-TIME ☐ FULL-TIME

19. IF YOU HAVE A PHYSICAL OR MENTAL IMPAIRMENT THAT SUBSTANTIALLY LIMITS A MAJOR LIFE ACTIVITY SUCH AS WALKING, TALKING, BREATHING OR WORKING, PLEASE EXPLAIN HERE:

20. WHERE ARE YOU WILLING TO WORK?	RELOCATE? ☐ Yes ☐ No	21. TYPING SPEED? WPM	22. RECEIVING WELFARE? ☐ YES ☐ NO	23. NUMBER IN FAMILY?	24. TOTAL ESTIMATED HOUSEHOLD INCOME OF LAST 6 MONTHS?

25. VETERANS AND OTHERS ELIGIBLE FOR VETERANS PREFERENCE: (CHECK APPROPRIATE BOXES)

☐ I CERTIFY THAT I SERVED ON ACTIVE DUTY IN THE U.S. ARMED FORCES FROM _____ TO _____ AND WAS DISCHARGED WITH OTHER THAN A DISHONORABLE DISCHARGE.

I HAVE A VA DISABILITY RATING OF: ☐ UNDER 30% ☐ 30% OR MORE ☐ DISCHARGED DUE TO SERVICE CONNECTED DISABILITY

☐ I AM NOT A VETERAN, BUT I AM ENTITLED TO VETERANS PREFERENCE (EXAMPLE - WIDOW).

SIGNATURE: _____

26. HAVE YOU BEEN CONVICTED OF A FELONY? (INCLUDING JUVENILE OFFENSES) ☐ YES ☐ NO	27. KIND OF WORK YOU ARE SEEKING? 1ST CHOICE: _____ 2ND CHOICE: _____

28. SKILLS, LICENSES, CERTIFICATES, MACHINES OPERATED, TOOLS OWNED, SHORTHAND SPEED, WORD PROCESSING, LANGUAGES, ETC.

PLEASE CONTINUE ON OTHER SIDE	DO NOT WRITE IN SHADED AREA	FOR OFFICE USE ONLY

A. REG TYPE   B. DOT

C. EMPL STAT   D. IN SCH   E. ETHNIC   F. MIN WAG

G. EDUC   H. DRIVE LIC   I. SHIFT   J. HANDI-CAPPED   K. LMID   L. SDA

M. SEC DOT   N. TYPING   O. VET   P. MSFW   Q. WEL-FARE

R. ECON DISAD   S. FELON   T. SRCH EXCL   U. ELIG GRP

V. UI CLM   SPECIAL RPT / CODE   W. RESTRICT TO EMPLOYER

X. TEMPORARY PHONE (___) ___ - ___

Y. FELONY _____

Z. HANDICAPPED: _____

AA. RESTRICTIONS: _____

BB. GEN NOTES: _____

CC. BATCH SRCH ☐

DE 2451 Rev. 4 (7-92)   State of California / Employment Development Department

92 64814

29. PLEASE DESCRIBE IN DETAIL THE JOB DUTIES OF YOUR THREE MOST IMPORTANT JOBS BEGINNING WITH MOST RECENT:

A.

JOB TITLE	START DATE (MO/DA/YR)	END DATE (MO/DA/YR)

COMPANY NAME	CITY	STATE

WAGES

$ _____ per ☐ HOUR ☐ DAY ☐ WEEK ☐ MONTH ☐ YEAR

FULL-TIME   ☐ YES ☐ NO

DUTIES

REASON FOR LEAVING

B.

JOB TITLE	START DATE (MO/DA/YR)	END DATE (MO/DA/YR)

COMPANY NAME	CITY	STATE

WAGES

$ _____ per ☐ HOUR ☐ DAY ☐ WEEK ☐ MONTH ☐ YEAR

FULL-TIME   ☐ YES ☐ NO

DUTIES

REASON FOR LEAVING

C.

JOB TITLE	START DATE (MO/DA/YR)	END DATE (MO/DA/YR)

COMPANY NAME	CITY	STATE

WAGES

$ _____ per ☐ HOUR ☐ DAY ☐ WEEK ☐ MONTH ☐ YEAR

FULL-TIME   ☐ YES ☐ NO

DUTIES

REASON FOR LEAVING

DO NOT WRITE IN SHADED AREA - FOR OFFICE USE ONLY

KEYWORDS	EX	ED	KEYWORDS	EX	ED

air. Or you quit because of intolerable work conditions; You experienced sexual harassment.

Tip 2: **Question 11.** Many people stumble on this question. If you check off "discharged" (fired), you signal to the unemployment office that you were at fault for losing your job. Don't get this term confused with "laid off" or "voluntarily quit" which indicate that you are not at fault for being unemployed.

Tip 3: **Question 12.** If you served in the armed forces or worked for the federal government, you will need to fill out a different set of forms.

Tip 4: **Question 13.** This question determines whether you might be receiving benefits from another state or another area in your state. You can't collect benefits in two places at the same time.

Tip 5: **Question 14.** If you are owed money from your past employer i.e. (back vacation pay), you won't receive benefits until you are no longer receiving any money.

Tip 6: **Question 15.** This question checks to see if you meet the able and available to work requirement. If you are not physically able to do your usual occupation, you may still receive benefits as long as you can do some other kinds of work. You will need to explain this at your interview.

Tip 7: **Question 16.** If you aren't immediately available for full-time work, you are not "available" and won't qualify for benefits.

Tip 8: **Question 17.** If you are planning to enroll in a training course or school, make sure you've checked that it's approved by the unemployment benefits office. If it's not approved, you are not available for work and will be denied benefits.

Tip 9: **Question 18.** As you learned in chapter two, if you are self-employed, you are not covered under this system. The one exception is in California where you might have paid into the system to be covered. One possible way around this is if you are still able to work full-time and are actively seeking work.

Tip 10: **Question 20.** If you are a member of a union, you must be registered as out-of-work with the union to qualify for benefits.

Tip 11: **Question 21.** If you are receiving pension money, your benefit amount will be reduced or you might be ineligible for benefits.

Form 2 —T ips

Tip 1: **Question 10.** Write down a figure similar to what you earned at your last job, otherwise the unemployment office may find that you are "unavailable" for work and don't qualify for benefits.

Tip 2: **Question 11.** You must be unemployed to receive benefits. In most states, even if you have a part-time job, you must be fully unemployed for at least one week.

Tip 3: **Question 12.** If you are in school full time, you will be denied benefits, unless you can show that the job you're looking for and are qualified for requires night-shift work.

Tip 4: **Question 17.** Write down the hours that you worked at your last job. If you've drastically changed your schedule—you're going to classes in the morning—you need to be sure that there are still jobs for which you are qualified during the hours that you are available. Otherwise, you will most likely be considered "unavailable" for work.

If the job that you are looking for requires you to work at night or to work on the weekends, you need to write down that you are available during these hours. For example, as a construction worker, you often work on the weekends and early mornings. If you can't work during those times, you will be considered "unavailable" and will most likely be denied benefits.

Tip 5: **Question 19.** Although businesses cannot discriminate against you because of a disability, you must show that you are qualified for a particular line of work. The law requires employers to provide you with reasonable accommodations to help you do your job. If you have a disability, write it down here and explain in your interview that you are qualified and are able to do a particular job.

Tip 6: **Question 20.** You don't have to search for work in other cities or counties, unless your former job was in a distant place. You don't have to be willing to travel an "unreasonable" distance to get a job or to relocate. Most states won't require you to travel much further than your last job. You can check past cases for what your state considers "unreasonable" traveling time. Go to any law library and ask for a series of books called *Precedent Decisions*. For more information about doing this research, read "Review Past Decisions" in chapter six on winning your appeal.

Tip 7: **Question 21.** Don't volunteer skills that have become obsolete. For example, you may have been able to type 100 words per minute twenty years ago, but if you write that down, the unemployment office may then question why you're not looking for work as a secretary or word processor now.

Tip 8: **Question 27.** You are asked to write down what kind of work you are looking for. The unemployment office is attempting to determine whether you've narrowed your job search to the point that you will almost never get hired. For example, if you were a carpenter and now you write down you are looking for work as a financial analyst at one of the top ten banks, you won't see a benefit check soon. You are making yourself unavailable for work, which is one of the criteria for eligibility (See chapter two and the "able and available" requirement).

Write down work in your field of knowledge and expertise, which, in most cases, will be the same kind of work that you did in your former job. You can also include other work you are considering, and, at your interview, you can explain how you are qualified to do this other work.

Tip 9: **Question 28.** When you explain that you have a carpenter's license, can operate a printing machine and can take shorthand, you will be expected to look for work in all those areas. If you are not qualified in shorthand, think twice before writing it down here.

Tip 10: **Question 29.** The unemployment office is only concerned about the reason why you left your last job. For the most recent job, which is the one that matters here, state simply and clearly why you left your last job. Follow the suggested answers given in the first question on form 1. The other two jobs are providing information about your skills and earning potential.

The Interview
When you pick up your forms from the unemployment insurance benefits office, you will also receive a date and time to be interviewed. The interview

takes place several days after you turn in your forms and register for work. Some states send you a notice in the mail confirming your interview. If the time and date is not suitable, contact the unemployment office immediately and reschedule.

The interview will be conducted either by phone or face-to-face. Be pleasant, but don't volunteer extra information. Keep your answers simple and concise. If you've read chapter two on eligibility, you have a sense of the kind of questions that you will be asked: Are you unemployed? If you aren't working and are not receiving a pay check, you are unemployed. If you work part-time, you may still be considered unemployed. Are you able to work? Are you available for work?

Judy made an offhand remark to her interviewer about considering a line of work other than waitressing. She was, however, continuing to look for jobs in the restaurant and service industry, the area she had worked in for over seven years. Yet she was denied benefits by the unemployment officer because she removed herself from the labor market. "And I thought I was making light conversation," said Judy at her appeal, two months later.

"Remember the interviewer is not your friend or confidant," said one employment attorney. "They are doing their job of gathering facts and are not there to take your side."

As you talk, the interviewer takes notes often called the "Notice of Claim Status Interview." Anything recorded on this paper tends to be regarded as fact in your case. Because the unemployment employees are busy, not a lot of time is allocated to verify your facts or the version of the facts given by your former employer. Before you let it go any farther, ask the interviewer to read back any of your more complex responses to clarify confusion. If Judy in the above example had asked the agent to read back her answers, she would have caught his error then, rather than being denied benefits and having to wait two months until her appeal hearing. Your interview, initial application, and your former employer's response, if any, are used to decide whether you receive benefits.

Check List for the Interview
❑ Remember: the interviewer is not your friend. Don't volunteer information. Be honest and be concise.

❑ If you have written documentation to back up your statements, bring those records. For example, if the workplace conditions were harming your health, bring your medical records or a letter from your doctor. If your employer laid you off and put it in writing, bring that form.

❏ Ask your interviewer to read back your answers if your responses were involved or complex.

❏ Don't argue with the interviewer.

Continued Claim Form

When you file for unemployment benefits, you must also start filing continued claim forms in most states. This form must be filled out and returned, usually every two weeks. It is typically mailed to you along with your benefits check which comes every two weeks. With this form, the unemployment office monitors your job search efforts. Some typical questions include: "Did you work this week?" and you check a box "yes" or "no." If you worked, you most likely must explain for whom. "Were you physically able to work full-time each day of the week?" And "Was any work offered to you during this week?" How you answer triggers a denial of your benefits if you fail to follow the rules. (See appendix for sample form).

If you take a part-time job while receiving benefits, some of this money will be deducted from your weekly benefit check. And if you are sick or unavailable, your check will be reduced.

During his second week of receiving benefits, Ethan, a former copy editor, received a job offer from a temporary agency as a secretary. The job was located downtown and involved heavy computer work. But Ethan suffers from carpal tunnel syndrome and he can't type for long periods of time during the day. "My doctor has written to the unemployment office and to the temp agency that I can't sit for eight hours and only type," said Ethan. He turned down the job offer and marked on his continued claim form that he refused a job. However, he failed to write down why he turned down the offer.

Two weeks later, the agency cut off his benefits and asked for a refund of the money paid to him for the last couple weeks, the time period when he would have been working had he taken the job. He filed an appeal. Through months of perseverance, he was able to win back his benefits. Be very careful when you mark down that you refused a job offer on your continued claim form. Explain precisely why you turned it down.

When Benefits Are Denied

If you are denied benefits after filing your initial claim form and completing your interview, you should immediately appeal. In chapter five, this process is fully explained.(See appendix for sample form).

The other alternative is to "purge" your disqualification by taking a temporary job or through serving a waiting period. Then, when this second job ends, refile your claim.

Suing Your Former Employer

Take a moment and reflect on how and why you lost your job to consider whether you have a possible lawsuit against your former employer. Although there isn't room here to talk about all the possible variations of lawsuits, read the descriptions below to decide whether you might have a suit. If there are similarities between what happened to you and these brief explanations of possible suits, you might consider meeting with a legal aid or a private attorney. After you describe your situation, an attorney will be better able to tell you whether you should sue.

Wrongful Discharge

If your employer fired you because you refused to perform an illegal act, your employer violated the law. You have been wrongfully discharged if you were fired because you did something that the law encourages or protects. For example, Jan was a bank teller and she saw that her manager consistently overcharged customers. When Jan informed the bank auditors about her employer's actions, she was fired. Jan was wrongfully discharged because her firing was a result of trying to get her boss to uphold the law.

If your former boss made oral and written promises to you about your job security and benefits, those promises will most likely be upheld by a court. So if your former boss promised to give you six months notice before dismissing you and he laid you off immediately, you probably have a wrongful discharge suit.

Joe was a salesman for forty years at a shoe manufacturing company. When he ended the year with the highest amount of commission ever, his boss fired him so that he wouldn't have to pay Joe the commission. Many courts would find that Joe was wrongfully discharged because his boss did not treat him fairly. In a California case, the court found that the employer violated the law when he dismissed a long-term employee without a hearing, as promised in the personnel handbook of policies.

If you do win a wrongful discharge suit, you can receive your back pay and lost benefits, damages, and you may be reinstated to your old job or an equivalent position in the company.

Anti-Retaliation Laws

If you were fired for reporting violations of laws or dangers to your health and safety at work, you may be able to sue and get your job back.

Discrimination

Laws preventing employment discrimination cover all aspects of your relationship to your boss: hiring, wages, benefits, evaluations, promotions, assignments, and firings. There is no requirement that any person be hired, regardless of her qualifications, simply because she is a member of one of the protected groups. What is required is that arbitrary, artificial, and irrelevant standards and practices be removed when they bar the employment and advancement on the job of protected groups such as women and minorities. There are very strict time limits for filing a lawsuit, so you must file right away. For more information about workplace discrimination and equal employment, call your local office of the federal Equal Employment Opportunity Commission. Also your local chapters of the American Civil Liberties Union (ACLU) and the National Association for the Advancement of Colored Persons (NAACP) can help answer your questions. You don't have to hire an attorney to bring an EEOC complaint.

Pregnancy

Your employer can't discriminate against you because you are pregnant. This ban covers all areas of employment—hiring, promoting, receiving seniority rights and fringe benefits, and firing. If you work around chemicals, and your employer dismisses you from your job, saying he is trying to protect the fetus from harm, he has discriminated against you. As long as you are as capable of doing your job as your male counterparts, you can't be dismissed on the basis of pregnancy or reproductive capacity.

Sexual Harassment

Your former boss must provide a workplace that is free of a biased atmosphere. Your employer violates the law when he permits supervisors or employees to act in sexually offensive ways, to intimidate you, or interfere with your work. If you thought that you'd lose your job or be denied a promotion or good work assignments unless you submitted to sexual overtures at work, then you were sexually harassed.

Age Discrimination
If you are forty years old or older, any decision that your former boss made must have been based on your ability or capacity to do your work, and not because you just turned fifty-five. If your company tried to increase productivity by firing all the older employees and keeping the younger ones, your company has violated the law.

Disability Discrimination
Your employer can't discriminate against you because of your disability. If you have a physical or mental impairment that substantially limits a major life activity—caring for yourself, walking, seeing, participating in community activities—you are considered disabled and protected by this law. If you have a record of this impairment or are regarded as having this impairment, you are considered disabled. If you have the Human Immunodeficiency Virus (HIV), you are considered disabled and protected from discrimination.

Job Safety Issues
Your employer is required to maintain a workplace free from recognized hazards to your health and safety. Some states also have "right to know" laws which require varying degrees of disclosure of information to you about the hazardous materials that you handle on the job. These laws are enforced by the Labor Department's Occupational Safety and Health Administration (OSHA). You have the right to report unsafe or unhealthy working conditions to OSHA and your employer can't punish or discriminate against you for doing this. If you are punished, you have a certain amount of time to contact and file a complaint with OSHA. If your employer fired you and OSHA determines that you were unlawfully punished, your employer will have to reinstate you and restore lost earnings and benefits.

Sources of Information and Help

Several national civil liberties and civil rights organizations have state and local offices throughout the United States. If you think you might have a discrimination complaint, you can contact an attorney from the following organizations by referring to the telephone directory or contacting these numbers:

- Mexican American Legal Defense and Education Fund
  182 2nd Street, San Francisco, CA 94105 (415) 543-5598.

- National Association for the Advancement of Colored People
  1397 Fulton Street, Brooklyn, NY 11217 (718) 789-3043
  NAACP legal defense and education fund.

- Local chapters of the American Civil Liberties Union.
  Check the telephone directory.

- National Urban League
  1111 14th Street, N.W. Washington, D.C. 20005 (202) 898-1604.

- Puerto Rican Legal Defense and Education Fund
  99 Hudson Street, 14th Floor, New York, NY 10013 (212) 219-3360.

- Native American Rights Fund
  1506 Broadway, Boulder, CO 80302 (303) 447-8760.

- Southern Poverty Law Center
  400 Washington Avenue, Montgomery AL 36104 (205) 264-0286.

- Women's Legal Defense Fund
  1875 Connecticut Avenue, NW Suite 710, Washington, D.C., 20009
  (202) 986-2600.

Chapter 5

Winning Your Appeal

J essica Crom waits in a small, beige room on the fourth floor of the Employment Development Department (EDD) building in San Francisco. Impeccably dressed in a pink blazer and a black skirt, Crom nervously studies her handwritten notes, preparing to defend herself against her former employer's charges of misconduct. The EDD denied Crom unemployment benefits based on her employer's accusations and Crom chose to appeal the decision. Crom filed for unemployment benefits nearly two months ago. She's sent out over forty-five resumes to prospective employers and has had six job interviews but is still unemployed. A couple of employers have shown some interest, but she hasn't heard yet. Although the benefits would amount to only $90 a week, that's almost enough to pay her rent. Yet because she lost her initial claim for benefits, she has yet to see a penny.

Crom has sold her car and some furniture for extra money, and, at age twenty-nine, has decided to get out of the waitressing business because the job prospects look grim. Instead, she is interested in retail clothing. "My friends always ask me for help when dressing for something special," said Crom. But now, she figures since she has an automatic right to appeal the unemployment office's denial of her benefits, she shouldn't turn down this chance for a little extra money. As she says, "I have nothing to lose."

Crom arrived early to her hearing to review her unemployment file and read her employer's reason for why she was fired. In a phone interview with an agent from the unemployment office, her employer insisted that she consistently acted rudely to customers and disobeyed his orders to serve a group of drunk customers on New Year's Eve. Crom knows that on only one occasion could her actions be considered rude. She writes this down because she doesn't want to forget to say this in the hearing. Things were so busy New Year's Eve that it took her forty-five minutes to finally take the orders from a group of ten. One of the ladies in the group who had drunk too much complained to Crom's boss.

A tall, black-robed administrative law judge (also called a referee or examiner) calls Crom's name, and she follows him into a small room. The judge moves quickly to the end of the long table and adjusts the tape recorder to tape the hearing. Crom's employer, the owner of the restaurant, sits across the table from her. The judge announces that he doesn't have a lot of time, nine more hearings after this one.

After both Crom and her employer accept the papers in the file as evidence, the judge signals for Crom's employer to begin the hearing by explaining why he fired Crom. He argues that she acted rudely to customers on a consistent basis. The judge interrupts him and asks for dates and how she acted rudely. Fumbling with papers, her employer says he isn't sure when or how. And he doesn't have any notes documenting whether he reprimanded her after the New Year's Eve incident. But he does know that she was rude that night.

Now, It's Her Turn

Crom tells the judge about the drunk table of ten. Crom said she had politely explained to the woman that she had to wait on ten other tables as well. Crom introduces her coworker, who confirms her story. The judge

asks Crom if she was rude to the lady. Crom answers no. He inquires whether her boss complained to her later about her performance. Crom answers no, that her boss understood it was a busy night. The judge asks her again if she was rude. Did she yell back, did she make a scene? No.

The judge asks her employer if he has anything else to say. He adds that Crom's performance at work was too poor to keep her.

Crom has a chance to respond. She introduces into evidence her job performance record which she had subpoenaed earlier from her boss. In that report, her manager gives her high marks as a waitress. "This shows that I performed well at my job," said Crom. Crom's witness also verifies that she was a hard worker. The judge then asks if either party has a closing statement. Crom checks her list of issues to address—everything covered, so she declines making any statement. The judge flicks off the tape recorder and collects his files and tapes. He tells Crom she must file continued claim forms for each week that she is unemployed. Even if she wins this appeal, he tells her, she must file these claims, or she won't win anything. He turns the page of his procedure manual, tells Crom that she should get a decision in the mail in three to four weeks, shuts his binder and marches through the front door.

With a stunned look, Crom makes a note to find out what "continued claim" forms are and gathers her things, not bothering to talk to her former boss.

As the prolonged recession hits one industry after another, over ten million Americans joined Crom in the long line for unemployment benefits during 1992. Hard hit by the recession, businesses are shedding employees to cut costs and match lackluster consumer demand. But with each firing, the leaner, meaner business is hit by a corresponding Catch-22 cost—unemployment benefits charges. Each time another employee is laid off and receives benefits, this former employer has to pay more money into a special fund (except Alaska, New Jersey, and Pennsylvania, where employees are required to share the cost). Money from that fund pays for your benefits. Sometimes, employers assemble an array of resources to fight your claim. There are management firms that specialize in defending employers against having to pay more money into the fund. More than ever, unemployment claims are likely to be contested or appealed by employers as businesses look for ways to cut costs.

If you are like the majority of people at this stage of the unemployment benefits process, you are left to face the employer's barrage alone. Few attorneys represent former employees at these hearings, because there is little money to be made. You may be able to receive legal advice from a legal aid clinic. Or if your case is unique with complicated facts, you may want to call your local bar association and have them refer you to a private attorney.

But most likely, it's up to you to present your case in the best light. It's your chance to make sure someone listens to both sides and carefully sifts through the facts. Over one-half of the states' laws provide that appeals at this stage are heard by a single judge or referee. (In the other states, an appeal may be heard by a referee and two associates, the associates representing the interests of employers and employees. However, everything which is said here applies to this situation as well).

Even if you initially win your benefits, you may receive a notice in the mail, stating that your employer is appealing the decision. When this happens, prepare for the hearing just as thoroughly as if you had initially been denied benefits and are fighting to win them. Then, you will be better able to meet whatever arguments your former employer raises.

If you received benefits after filing your initial claim form, you will continue to collect them until the decision on the appeal is made. If you lose the appeal, you may be required to pay back the benefits.

When Jessica Crom received the letter, called a "notice of determination" (or ruling, or local office decision), denying benefits to her, she almost chose not to appeal. Already overwhelmed with her job search— going to interviews, researching jobs at the library, and attending a career center service—Crom didn't think she could carve out enough time to appeal as well. Although she thought she qualified to receive benefits, maybe the unemployment agents knew more about the law than she did. Maybe making her customers wait forty-five minutes meant misconduct. At the last moment, though, she filed anyway because, like she said, what did she have to lose?

Fortunately, Crom listened to her common sense. There are good reasons why you should go ahead and appeal:

- It's a chance to present your side to a human being who is trained in sorting through the facts of the situation and making a fair decision— for free. Every state is required to provide a fair hearing if your benefits are denied.

- A mistake on your initial claim form might have been the reason that you were denied benefits. For example, if you indicated that you were "terminated" versus "laid off," this might be enough of a reason for the unemployment agent to deny you benefits. With a simple explanation at the appeals hearing about how you were laid off because business was slow, you could have some of the financial burden of unemployment eased with a weekly check.

- If you show up to the hearing and your employer does not, you have a definite advantage. You can present your version of the facts without your employer countering it.

- The appeals judge/referee will help you in presenting your case, especially if your employer has an attorney present. Your referee is required to give you a fair and impartial hearing.

- The hearing takes anywhere from ten minutes to several hours and it's free. You could end up winning several thousand dollars. If you don't take this opportunity now, even if you have the best case possible, you will not receive any money.

- More than one-third of the people who challenge the denial of their benefits win after a hearing. The success rate is much higher for those who are prepared.

- You may have been denied benefits because your former employer described your dismissal in less than accurate terms. The unemployment agent who interviews both you and your former employer does not have the time or resources to verify everything your boss says. What might have been carelessness on your part—making mistakes in a couple letters or forgetting to mail a letter—can easily be described by your boss as misconduct: you intentionally forgot to mail an important letter or you meant to make mistakes in the letters so that your former employer looked bad, neither of which are necessarily true.

You Can Appeal

If you are denied benefits, you will receive an official notice in the mail, a notice of determination or ruling or local office decision (see sample on page 133 in appendix). Read this form carefully because the reason for your denial will be clearly given here. This reason will be the main focus of your argument at the appeals hearing. For example, if the letter says that you were denied benefits because of absences from work, you must show at the hearing that you were late only occasionally and your boss never mentioned that it was a problem, or you were late for two weeks because of a sick child and you had received your employer's approval to be late. In that case, you wouldn't tell the judge or referee that you worked overtime for three weeks in a row. Nor do you need to argue that you have a great sales record or that your supervisor hates you. These explanations aren't addressing the reason for your denial: you were late for two weeks. Keep your argument focused on the legal issue.

Also on this notice (the letter denying you benefits) is the number of days you have to file an appeal. In most states, it will read twenty days from the date of the notice. Mark this date down now. If you are not sure of the time limit, file the appeal immediately. If you miss the deadline, some states allow you to file anyway, but it is extremely difficult to drudge up a good excuse that will allow you to appeal beyond the deadline. If you do miss the deadline, the best excuse is that you did not receive the notice within the twenty day period.

The Appeal Form

Your local appeals or unemployment office provides a standard appeal form. (See the appendix on page 134 for a sample form.) It will either be sent to you in the notice letter denying your benefits, or you can pick it up at the unemployment or appeals office. You need to fill it out and return it to the unemployment office. In most states, you must also file continued claim forms—one every week—until a final decision is made, or you won't receive the benefits owed to you, even if you win your appeal. (See page 135 for a sample form.)

The appeal form will ask for your name, address, and reason for appealing. Be clear and concise. Don't offer any additional information and be careful not to contradict information you gave on your initial claim form. A simple reason for appealing that most likely is acceptable is: "I don't agree with the decision."

Instead of mailing it, take the form down to the unemployment office so that you are sure you make the deadline. If your appeal is filed properly, the agency will send you a hearing notice confirming your ap-

peal. In some states, it's called the "notice of hearing." (See sample in appendix on page 136.) It will give the date, time, and place of the hearing. If you don't receive this notice within three weeks after you filed a request for an appeal, immediately call the unemployment office and ask. If you can't make the time set for the hearing, call the unemployment office to reschedule. If you wait until the last minute to try and reschedule, it probably won't happen. If you need an interpreter, notify the office of appeals immediately and one will be provided for you at no cost.

Preparing for Your Appeal

Now that you've received the time and day of your appeal, you should begin to prepare. Depending on the complexity of your case, you will need to do some or all of the following tasks to fully explain to the referee the facts surrounding your unemployment. Try explaining what happened to a friend. If your friend is confused, it may mean that you will need to work a little harder—maybe use witnesses or documents to explain your version to the referee.

When you are seated at the hearing table, the referee will ask you to swear to tell the truth, the whole truth, and nothing but the truth. When you answer "yes," everything you say after that is under oath and can then be used in a later trial or court proceeding. At first glance, you might think that the closest you will ever come to another encounter with the law is filing your taxes. But if you think you've been unfairly fired (called a "wrongful discharge") or you have experienced some kind of discrimination at your former job, you may have a lawsuit against your employer (See chapter four for a description of wrongful discharge or discrimination on the job.) After discussing your situation with a lawyer or a legal aid attorney, you will have a better idea whether you should file a suit. If the attorney says you have a strong case and agrees to represent you, most likely she will also represent you at the benefits hearing because the statements you make there can be used later in court—against you, if you say the wrong things.

Review Your File

When Crom decided to file her appeal, she called the appeals office and made an appointment to review her unemployment benefits file. In it, she found a detailed statement of the unemployment office's reasons for denying her application. She saw that her employer told the unemployment agent that she repeatedly insulted customers. She wrote that down because she felt that wasn't true. She also saw that her employer said she had a bad attitude. Crom didn't think that this was a legitimate reason for denial of her benefits. She wrote this down too. She also found a job performance evaluation that her employer must have sent the unemployment office. Although a poor evaluation, when Crom read the name at the top, it was for another employee. She wrote this down. Slowly, Crom began to piece together the argument she would make before the appeals judge.

Crom also made a chronology of events involving her firing. By now, she'd figured out that her employer argued she intentionally caused a disruption at his business by acting improperly with customers. Crom's job at the hearing would be to counter this, and only this.

In this chapter, you will find ways to argue your case, depending on if you were fired for misconduct, voluntarily quit your job for personal reasons or for work-related reasons.

Subpoena Work Documents and Your Coworkers
She made a list of what she needed to present her case. Since she had to show that she hadn't provided poor service, she decided to subpoena her job performance records. For three years now, she had received high marks from her manager. She also wanted to subpoena her old time cards, showing that she often covered for other employees who wanted time off. Finally, she included on her list to subpoena her coworker, who also had worked at the restaurant for four years. Her coworker was there on New Year's Eve and could explain that it was a chaotic night, with all tables taken, and that all the waitresses and waiters found it difficult to serve a table immediately when the customers sat down.

The unemployment office provides free subpoena forms called "subpena duces tecum," used to obtain documents. (The legal term for a subpoena requesting documents.) There's a sample form in the appendix on page 137. A subpoena is a piece of paper that tells someone to show up or bring something to a specific place at a certain time and date. If the subpoenaed person does not appear, she is liable for certain penalties. When asking for documents, the subpoena is served on the person who has the documents. Ask for the subpoena form as soon as possible and fill it out there. Then ask the appeals clerk to have a judge sign it to make it legal. You need to be ready to explain to the judge why you need the documents or the witnesses. A valid explanation might be, "My coworker can verify that I worked hard at my job which is the legal issue in my case." or "My coworker can tell the judge about the poor working conditions."

After you've explained, the judge will make her decision. The subpoena must be delivered to the person who has the documents in his possession or the person who you'd like to attend the hearing. Often, the office of appeals will serve the person by mail. Sometimes, your witness will agree to show up without a subpoena summoning her to the hearing. In this case, Crom would serve the subpoena on her old employer to obtain her evaluation records. She would also serve the subpoena on her coworker to attend the hearing.

Be aware that subpoenaing fellow employees to testify on your behalf is an uphill battle. In most cases, the employees who know the most are still working for the employer. It's hard to get them to show up. Their jobs are at stake. Even if they do show up, they may lie to keep their jobs.

Before relying on your coworker to help strengthen your case at the hearing, meet with her and talk about what she might say. Go over the questions you intend to ask and the issues that will most likely be raised at the hearing. In addition to your questions, your coworker will have to answer any questions asked by the referee or your former employer, if the questions are appropriate. After rehearsing awhile, you may decide at this early stage that you don't want your coworker to attend the hearing. This decision is better made before the hearing than in the middle of the person's testimony at your appeal.

When Tom attended his hearing, he wished he had subpoenaed his work performance record because he had received excellent reviews for three consecutive years from his former employer. He mentioned his evaluation at the hearing to defend himself against a charge of misconduct. But when the referee asked his boss about it, his former employer answered that he couldn't remember such a record. After the hearing concluded, Tom tried to tell the referee about the record, but since the hearing was over, there was nothing to be done. The referee suggested that if Tom chose to appeal again, to try and introduce it to the second level of appeal, the appeals board. "But it's very difficult to explain why you weren't prepared at this stage," the referee told Tom. Remember, this hearing is your big chance to tell your side of the story. Be prepared.

Use an Affidavit

The second best alternative to a subpoena if your coworker can't make it to the hearing, is a sworn affidavit. A sworn affidavit is a signed, written statement from your coworker or any other witness that tells the referee what your witness would say if she went to the hearing. A sworn affidavit, unlike a regular affidavit, includes: "I swear under penalty of perjury that the foregoing is true and correct." Make sure you include this statement, otherwise the affidavit won't help you. You can get free affidavit forms from the appeals office which is most likely near the unemployment office, or you can just use a plain sheet of paper. When your witness fills out the form, she will include her name, the date, a statement, and a signature. Affidavits are most valuable to you if the person telling their version of the facts has no reason to slant her testimony in your favor. For example, if you'd like the referee to hear from your doctor, in addition to a medical report, a sworn affidavit of his comments may help your case.

But remember, even though affidavits are easier to obtain than personal attendance, it is the latter that is given more significance by the judge.

Review Past Decisions

Every law library and some appeals offices (usually located near the unemployment office) where your hearing will be held have books filled with summaries of past cases that were heard in your state. Ask for a recent volume called *Precedent Decisions.* In this book are decisions made by the appeals board about unemployment benefits cases, some of which are similar to yours. The decisions are bound and published by the appeals board along with an index digest. Look under the index and locate the area that applies to you. For example, if you are unclear about whether you are eligible for benefits if you voluntarily quit your job because no one but you could care for your spouse, check under "eligibility" in the index. Then look under "voluntary quit."

Before Jessica Crom went to her hearing, she found a case just like hers that used what is called a "single instance" defense. She read in the case that this defense means that if you were careless on just one occasion, it's typically not enough of a reason to deny you benefits. She decided that this is how she should present her argument to the judge. She made a copy of the decision to bring with her to the hearing.

Watch a Hearing

Every day, judges are listening to appeals similar to the one you may be presenting. Ask the clerk or the judge if you can watch a hearing. Explain that your hearing is coming up soon, and you want to be prepared. Most likely, the judge will ask the people involved in the case if they would be bothered with you there. In some states, these hearings are public so you can go anytime and listen.

Have Someone Represent You

If your case is complicated or if there is another possible lawsuit that could be filed against your employer—wrongful discharge, discrimination, or harassment lawsuit—you should consider talking to an attorney about representing you. At the very least, if you have little income, meet with a legal aid attorney to go over your case. If you have some money, call your state bar office and ask for a referral to an attorney who does work in this area. If you belong to a union, a union attorney most likely will help you if your case is complex or an important one to the union.

Most attorneys agree, though, that the unemployment benefits system is set up so that you can represent yourself. The referee takes an active role at the hearing to help you cover the important information and make sure that you are given a fair hearing.

Write Down Your Arguments

Make an outline of your argument before you go into the hearing. List everything you want to be sure to say, remembering to stick to the legal reason why you were denied benefits. If you did extra research and found a past case similar to yours, include those notes and the number of that decision so that you can bring it to the judge's attention. If possible, bring a photocopy of the case to the hearing as well. In this chapter, you will find ways to argue your case, depending on if you were discharged for misconduct, voluntarily quit for personal reasons, or work-related reasons.

At Your Appeal Hearing

Depending on how complicated your case is, you've now completed some or all of the preparatory steps listed above. Your hearing date is around the corner, but before you go and dazzle the referee with your argument, read the following suggestions to make sure your hearing goes smoothly.

Arrive Early

Arrive thirty to forty minutes early to review your unemployment file one more time. Make sure that you are familiar with everything in it for two important reasons. First, the judge will ask you if you accept everything in it as evidence. If you agree, this means that the judge will consider all the information in the file to make her decision. And if you need to appeal again (assuming you live in a state where you can appeal a second time), the appeals board, the second level of appeal, will consider it, too. Normally, this won't be a problem. Any inaccurate statements made by your employer to the unemployment agent when you first filed your benefits claim can be countered by you at the hearing. A transcript is made of this hearing and given to the appeals board to consider, if you appeal again.

The second reason to take one more look at your file is to make sure your employer hasn't changed or added to his argument why you should be denied benefits. If this happens, you need to think fast and develop some new arguments for yourself. Add these new points to your list.

If the clerk will not give you your file, tell the referee that you were not allowed to see it. This may be grounds for an appeal from the hearing itself.

If you don't show up at your hearing, your appeal will be dismissed. To reopen your hearing, you must establish good cause for your failure to appear—you were very ill, a child was very ill and you are the only caretaker.

Dress Well

Although you don't follow formal rules for introducing your argument and evidence at this hearing, it is a formal court hearing. You should be neat and dress up for your presentation. Refer to the judge as "your honor."

Use Your Argument

The outline of your argument is crucial now. Hopefully, you've made an outline of the points you want to raise that directly address why you were denied benefits. List the documents, if any, you want to show the judge. Many people become nervous at the hearing, forgetting to cover everything they want to say or repeating the same point again and again. During the hearing for Ann, an unemployed retail salesperson, she kept saying over and over, "I've always done a good job. Look at my sales figures." She kept trying to show the judge her sales volume for the last three years. Yet her employer had argued that she had been fired for stealing. Whether she did a good job or not had nothing to do with the charge of misconduct. With your outline, you will be prepared to present your side.

When you give your version of the facts, glance down at your list and check off those items that you've covered. Try not to ramble or offer additional information.

Don't Interrupt

When your former employer presents his argument, don't interrupt. Write down your objections so that you can address them when you get another turn to explain your side.

Your strong feelings about your former employer or even the judge will not help build your case. Unable to control your anger because of the way your boss fired you, you may be tempted to oppose every single point the other side is making. But this leads to disaster. Your legal argument gets buried or completely lost in your angry outbursts.

Be Calm

This may be easier said than done. Make your arguments clearly and dispassionately. (See chapter six to help you handle the stress of this situation).

Maintain Eye Contact

Maintain as much eye contact as possible. Don't read your answers from your list of points because it will make you appear less believable. Just glance at your paper briefly, then look up and make your point.

Ask for Clarification

If you aren't sure what the judge is asking, ask him to explain. Don't guess in your answers—either be sure of what you're saying or admit that you don't know.

Make Copies

Make copies of any documents—time cards, affidavits, photos, job evaluations—that you want to give the judge. Make sure you have a copy for your employer, too. If the judge doesn't ask for evidence at the beginning of the hearing, you should introduce your documents when they are being discussed by you or by your witnesses. Make sure you refer to the documents in your testimony. For example, if you voluntarily left your job because the work conditions aggravated a medical condition, refer to the statement and medical report completed by your doctor.

Question Your Employer's Witness

After you and your former employer have spoken, the judge will give each of you an opportunity to ask questions of the other. This is called cross-examination. If you've ever watched a movie that included an important trial scene, this is the chance when an attorney for one side rifles into a witness for the other side. "So you were in the neighborhood on the night of the murder, weren't you? You were very close to 1234 Harbor Road, weren't you? In fact, you were in the very house where the murder was committed, weren't you?" You can feel the suspense building and the trap being set.

Although this may sound like fun, this is *not* what you are going to do. The only time you want to ask questions of the other side is when they have left out facts that are helpful to your case which they most likely can't deny. The paramount rule here is: If you don't know what to ask, don't ask. If you ask open-ended questions for which you don't know the answer, you give your employer's witness a chance to highlight points against you. "A common mistake is preparing only to smear the good name of your opponent," said William DeMartini, chief administrative law judge in California. "If you wish to win the appeal you should concentrate your efforts on the legal issues which control eligibility."

Don't Leave Things Out

Don't leave out information that you previously gave during your initial claim interview or on any forms you've filed so far. Resubmit all this information at the hearing. If you lose this appeal, you can appeal again in most states; all the information you present at your hearing will be typed up into a transcript. That's why the tape recorder is playing at the hearing. At the second appeal level, the appeals board will look at the transcript to help make their decision.

Closing

At the end of the hearing, the referee will ask you and your former employer if you have a closing statement. If anything remains on your checklist that you haven't raised, say it now. But if you've discussed everything, don't be repetitive.

The Decision

The hearing has ended and now you're back home checking your mailbox each day for the judge's decision, feeling like a hungry bird hunting for worms before winter. In about two or three weeks after the hearing, you will receive the decision, which will be based on information that was presented at the hearing and included in the unemployment office file. The decision will set forth (1) the issues and the facts that the judge found to be true after evaluating the evidence; (2) the law that the judge used; and (3) the conclusions and decision of the judge.

If you receive a favorable decision and have continued to look for work and to submit continued claim forms (if required by your state), you should receive a weekly benefit check. If you were initially denied benefits, you haven't received any money yet. Now, since you won, you will get a check for the amount of money had you initially been granted benefits. If you want to receive your money quicker, take a copy of the decision to the nearest unemployment office and ask them to help you.

How to Argue Your Appeal

If you were denied benefits and are now appealing that decision, you've learned that you need to present an argument to the referee, who will listen to the facts and decide whether you should receive benefits.

Voluntary Quit

- Personal Health Reasons: If you voluntarily quit your job because work conditions caused or aggravated a health problem, you should get a confirmation from your doctor. A letter will do, or a medical report signed by your doctor. If you can't afford a doctor, explain that to the judge. Write down some of the rates that the doctors quoted you and show that to the judge at the hearing.

    Also, if you tried to resolve the problem with your employer, make sure you mention this at the hearing. Or explain why it was pointless to try to work it out. For example, someone else tried to get your former boss to remove some of the toxic chemicals, but nothing happened.

- Domestic Reasons: If you leave your job to marry someone in another city, or to move with your spouse, you should try to show that it's too difficult to commute to your job from the new location. Document the mileage and hours. Make sure you've also written down how long it used to take you to get to work before you were married. Also, if you asked for a transfer but were denied, show the documentation.

Remember, if you've moved to a new state to be with your spouse, you file everything with the unemployment office in your new state. That office will send everything back to the previous state where you used to live.

- Sick Relative or Child: Make sure you document your efforts to find another alternative to quitting your job. Show the nursing facilities you called, as well as the prices quoted to you. Also be ready to explain why your spouse or relative can't do the caretaking. Subpoena your relative or have your spouse come with you as a witness to explain why you must be the caretaker. Also show why your former employer would not give you a leave of absence.

  The same argument goes for child care. Make a list of the day care centers that you called and the prices they charge. Explain why your spouse can't care for the kids and why you could not get a leave of absence.

- Intolerable Work Conditions: As described in chapter two on eligibility, examples of this reason for leaving are constant sexual harassment or use of offensive language. Proving that these conditions existed, however, is difficult. Your most valuable evidence are coworkers, but they are most likely still working for your old boss and don't want to risk losing their job by saying anything critical.

  Write down the occasions when you tried to talk with your employer about the problem. Or, if it would have been pointless to discuss the conditions with your boss, explain why. If a former employee who used to work with you now works at another job, she may be willing to testify at the hearing. If you filed a complaint about your employer's behavior with a government agency (Equal Employment Opportunity Commission, the Occupation Safety and Health Administration, or your union) bring a copy of this complaint to the hearing.

- Changes in Your Job: If you have taken a wage cut, check the past decisions of your state to determine what percentage reduction is

large enough to qualify as a good cause for leaving your job. Write down that case name so you can tell the judge. Also do this if you suffer major negative changes in your duties, hours, or benefits.

If your employer promised you something—a promotion, more hours, more pay—and fails to deliver, so you quit, you must be ready to show several things. First, unless the promise is written down, it will be difficult to prove: it's your word against your former boss'. Also, you should show that the promise helped you decide to take the job and how you've been injured because the promise was broken.

- Travel Problems: At the hearing, show how much time it takes to get to and from work. Bring maps and bus schedules to show the judge that there are no shorter routes. Be prepared to talk about how long it used to take you to go to work before your company moved its facilities or you moved your residence. Take a look at past decisions for your state and find out how long the commute has to increase to qualify for benefits. Photocopy the case if it helps you make your argument.

- Religious Reasons: You should be able to explain why your work violates your religion. If you can, bring someone from the church as your witness to testify. You also must show that the difficulties arose after you took the job: you can't start a job knowing that it conflicts with your religion and then quit and receive benefits.

- Remember to Notify: Always try and notify your employer of the problem before you leave your job. Try and work things out before quitting. Otherwise, you will be risking disqualification when your former boss responds at the hearing that he didn't know there was a problem. If you forgot to notify your boss, you may be able to argue (assuming it's true) that it would have been futile to mention it to your boss, because he wouldn't have done anything anyway. Be ready to give past examples of your boss not responding to problems.

- Leave of Absence: Read your company employment policy handbook and find out about the leave of absence policy. If you have one at your company, request a leave rather than choosing to quit. If your employer agrees, you will then get your job back after the leave of absence runs out. Get your leave of absence in writing so that there will be no disputes upon your return.

If your employer agrees to give you a leave of absence, you will receive benefits if your job is not available when you return. In this case, bring your written leave of absence note with you to the hearing.

If you didn't ask for a leave of absence, show that even if you had asked, it would have been denied. Show that other people have been denied a leave of absence for a reason you were asking for a leave.

Misconduct

If you were denied benefits (or received them and your employer has appealed) because of misconduct, you will use different arguments than if you voluntarily quit. Remember, the key here is that your former boss must show that you acted intentionally. This is more than acting carelessly or being incompetent.

Insubordination: The judge is most likely looking to see if there has been a pattern of insubordination—repeated acts of failing to do your job as required or consistently exceeding your job responsibilities. If the judge finds a pattern of insubordination, you could argue (if it's true) that your boss never gave you any warnings or reprimands, but let the action happen again and again. How could you be intentionally hurting your employer's business when he never told you to stop?

At your hearing, you should explain that you did not refuse to follow your boss's rules or requests; or if you did refuse, you should explain why your boss's request was not a reasonable one. For example, there was an emergency, and you had to take care of it rather than answer the phones. Or perhaps you didn't understand that your boss needed the work done right away. Maybe a coworker told you to do something, relaying a message from your boss, but you thought it was just your coworker ordering you around.

Or you can argue that your failure to follow the rule or the request did not cause substantial damage to your employer's business.

Another way to argue is to show that your employer allowed other employees to act similarly. For example, a construction worker was fired for tardiness. He subpoenaed all the time cards for other workers of the company, which showed that almost every other employee consistently showed up late for work. The judge reversed, and he received his benefits.

Tardiness/Absenteeism: You should tell the judge that you never received warnings (if this is true), so you were led to believe that your behavior was acceptable. Or, if you were tardy one or two times, you may be able to argue that you did not hinder your employer's business. If you were ill, tell the judge: This is not intentional conduct as long as you notified your boss before missing work days.

Dishonesty: One employment attorney suggested that you argue that you had your boss's property in your possession by mistake, and not because of theft.

Whether you alleged acted dishonestly or failed to follow your boss' rules, you should emphasize that your actions never rose to the level of misconduct: you carelessly moved the boxes and a couple happened to spill, breaking the glass vases inside. Your employer probably doesn't know the difference between his preferences for job performance and legal misconduct. He just knows that you did something he didn't like, so you shouldn't be rewarded with benefits. Insist that you did the best that you could, and although your employer may think you are incompetent, you worked hard. Remember, in most states, the key element that the employer must prove is that you acted intentionally.

If you did drop the boxes and break everything inside, point out to the judge that it only happened one time. You've moved boxes for seven years, and this is the only time a set happened to fall. As long as your carelessness did not cause major damage to your former employer, a one time act of incompetence will most likely not be considered misconduct.

Sometimes there is another reason for your firing, other than the misconduct that your employer has argued. One way to show that the misconduct was not the real reason for the discharge is to point out the timing between the act and the actually firing. If you were fired long after the misconduct, this could suggest to the judge that there was another reason.

Able and Available

As you learned earlier in chapter two, you must be able and available for work to be eligible for benefits.

To defend yourself against a charge that you are not able and available, make sure that you keep detailed lists of where you apply to work, the number of resumes sent out, and job seminars and fairs that you attend. You are trying to show that the jobs that you are looking for exist and are available and that you've been actively searching for a job. You are also establishing that you haven't limited yourself too much to a particular field or hours that make it difficult to find a job.

Suitable Work

The job offer must be for a real job that actually exists. You could argue that not enough details about the job were given to you, so you couldn't determine if the job was suitable for you. To help you appeal this decision, take a look at some past cases in the *Precedent Decisions* book and find similar cases to yours. See if the arguments used in the past cases will fit your facts.

Judy refused a job offer because she would have to work weekends, and she couldn't find child care for her one-year-old during that time. In that case, the judge said that as long as she was willing to work during the weekdays in a wide variety of jobs, she would not be disqualified from receiving benefits.

Jan took classes in the morning and was willing to work during the days and evenings. So when she was offered a job to work in the morning, she turned it down. The judge found that Jan had the necessary skills for many different jobs that would not require her to work while in school, so she still qualified for benefits.

Interstate Claims

If you've moved to another state since you've lost your job, you will be filing an interstate claim. If you are denied benefits by your former state, you will receive a notice stating the reasons why you were denied. It will also give you a date by which you must file an appeal.

At your hearing, your argument will be taped by a referee in your new state and sent back to your former state. Then, a referee from your old state will listen to the tape and make her decision. If all your witnesses live in your former state, write them and ask them to send an affidavit to you. Then, present the affidavits to the referee in the new state.

The Second Appeal

If you are unhappy with the decision from the appeals referee, you have a certain amount of time to file a second appeal (except in Hawaii, the Virgin Islands, or Nebraska, which have no second level of appeal). This

second level of appeal is heard by something called a board of review, board of appeals, or appeals board. In this section, the names will be used interchangeably. In Hawaii, Michigan, Ohio, and Tennessee, the referee/judge who heard your first appeal may reconsider her decision within the appeal period. Nebraska law allows the referee to reopen the appeal decision upon request within ninety days of the date of mailing on the basis of fraud, mistake, or new evidence. In Puerto Rico and Rhode Island, the decision of the appeals referee may be reopened if an employee or employer has been defrauded or coerced in connection with the decision.

In all other states, send a written request to the appeals board asking for another appeal. The board will send a letter which acknowledges receipt of your appeal and informs you and your employer of your rights and obligations.

The appeals board typically does not accept new evidence or claims not already introduced at the earlier appeal hearing, unless you can show that you could not have found or received your new evidence at the time of your first appeals hearing. In most states, however, you can submit a written argument to restate your case.

The information that the appeals board looks at most closely, however, is the transcript from the appeals hearing and the interviews conducted with you and your employer when you first filed the claim.

Preparing the Second Appeal

Vera worked as a temporary secretary and her employers included several temp agencies. When the agencies didn't have any work for her, they laid her off and she collected unemployment benefits. Then, on a Monday, one of her temp agencies called with a job offer. They explained the job location and that she would be doing heavy typing for eight hours a day. When Vera tried to explain that she couldn't do heavy typing because of her back, the temp agency hung up.

For that week, then, on her continued claim form, Vera marked down that she declined a job offer because of her medical condition. The next week, her benefits were cut off. She appealed the decision and the judge said that she should have taken the job.

But Vera believed that the judge made a mistake. She carefully read the notice that explained why she was denied benefits and saw that the judge focused on only one aspect of her argument. She had mentioned two things at the hearing: the job involved heavy typing, which her doctor said she couldn't do and that she did not feel safe in the neighborhood where the job was located. The judge only considered the latter reason and denied her benefits. On the notice she also saw that she had twenty days (check with your state to find out how long you have) to appeal this decision.

She obtained an appeal form from the unemployment benefits office and ordered the transcript from her first hearing. She mailed her request to the local office of appeals which issued the first decision. She included her case number assigned by the local office, her name, social security number, and the date of the hearing. She also requested permission to submit a written argument to the board.

Now Vera sought help to write the written argument. She attended a legal aid clinic and met with a law student. As the student explained, the written argument must be confined to the information already presented to the unemployment officer or the appeals judge.

"There are three ways to go here," explained the student. "Either we argue that the judge didn't apply the law correctly. Or the judge mishandled the process (he didn't let you introduce evidence that was important to your case). Or all the information that was in your file fails to support the facts that the judge relies on to make his decision." They decided to take the last tactic. Vera and the student wrote an argument that Vera had introduced medical records and a letter from her doctor informing the judge that she couldn't take a job that involved heavy typing, but the judge's decision didn't mention that fact. Instead, the judge only considered that she felt unsafe in the neighborhood, even though she didn't visit the area.

After three weeks passed, she called the board and inquired about her transcript, making sure that the office had her correct home address. One week later, she received the transcript and permission to submit her written argument.

So far, Vera has done everything she can to appeal her denial of benefits. To insure that the last level of appeal goes smoothly, here are a few things you can do:

❑ Check the time frame for filing an appeal.

❑ Request permission to submit a written argument (if this is allowed in your state).

❑ Request a transcript from your first appeal hearing.

❑ If you decide to write a written argument, try and meet with a legal aid assistant or law student to help you write it.

After a month and a half, Vera opens her mailbox. There, she finds a letter from the appeals board. She rips it open. The board says that it agrees with her, that she should continue to receive benefits. In two weeks, she will receive her check.

Superior Court

You've made it this far in the process, how about one more round? If you lost in your second appeal and think that you've got a good argument why you should receive your benefits, you can take your case to the state court system. This time, though, there will be more expense, because you are now moving out of the unemployment and appeals system and into the regular courts, where you need an attorney to represent you. Before you continue fighting for your benefits, if you haven't met with a legal aid attorney or a private attorney, now is the time. An attorney can listen to your situation and determine whether it's worth the time and expense to keep fighting.

You might have a lawsuit against your employer because you were fired, violating an employment contract that said you would work for a year. Or you might have a lawsuit because of the way you were treated on the job—a sexual harassment claim or age discrimination claim. Most attorneys will be interested in your case because there is big money to be earned with these kinds of suits.

6 Handling the Job Hunt

hough the company's projects had dwindled to three, landscape architect Jennifer Skinner barely noticed. After only three years at the firm, Skinner had moved quickly into a position of responsibility, knee-deep in important designs for a business park center, an urban park, and a garden for a low-income apartment building. Her thoughtful design of a senior citizens park, with bocci ball courts and a sensory garden, hung in the office lobby. In her drawing, she included raised vats so that the elderly would not have to stoop to plant vegetables.

When her company lost its contract to redesign a large business park, Skinner allocated more time to polishing her other projects. Although several people already had been laid off, Skinner was unprepared for her own dismissal on the following Monday morning.

"These things are always a shock when they actually happen to you," said Skinner. Instead of venting her emotions at the office, she explained she needed time before she could discuss her severance package. She made an appointment for the next day and quickly left. Skinner wanted to be calm to assess her health care needs, severance pay, and job search requirements. She needed to draw up a six-month budget, since she figured it would take that long to find a new position. She knew also that her boss would be an important reference for her next job.

Skinner's initial reaction of shock and anger marks the first loop of an emotional roller coaster set into motion by job loss.

The Emotions Involved with Job Loss

"Losing your job is like any other loss," said Lesah Beckhusen, a career consultant with an outplacement company. Beckhusen uses an inverted bell curve to illustrate the emotions associated with loss. Instead of a smooth line, it's curvy, with extreme highs and intense lows forming the shape of an upside-down bell. Very rarely will someone proceed in a smooth linear line through the different emotional stages. "It's much more up and down, backward and forward," said Robin Holt, a career counselor. For example, sending out a resume can take a tremendous amount of determination and energy. Receiving a rejection letter from a potential employer may result in deep depression.

Women's reaction to losing a job is often very different from men's. A man's identity is much more likely to be derived from his job, salary, and the power that he wields. A job loss sends him scurrying to find another as soon as possible. A woman's identity, especially those in clerical or service jobs, on the other hand, is often more closely tied to satisfying relationships. A job loss can throw her into an examination of her relationships, her career choice, and the balance between various facets of her life. "As a result, women who are not on a career path and who have not adopted the male approach to work often take longer to move from one job to the next," said Charles Prugh, an outplacement and career consultant. "It's a much more personal self-exploration."

Another explanation for the difference is that men tend to externalize the reason why they lost their job whereas women tend to internalize. In her book, *Games Mother Never Taught You,* Betty Lehan

Harragan writes, "Men too suffer disappointments during a long business career, but their reactions are qualitatively different. As a rule, they are not dumbfounded by their experience. Their response is more likely summed up as 'I knew the bastard would do this to me if he ever got the chance.' They foresee outcomes, understand why something happens, accept consequences. They are seldom crushingly surprised."

To illustrate the impact of the job loss, Dr. Thomas Holmes at the University of Washington School of Medicine developed a numerical scale rating life events associated with varying amounts of disruption in an average person's life. The higher the rating, the more stressful the event. Death of a spouse ranks 100, marital separation, 65, and being fired from a job is 47.

"The point is, you are supposed to feel lousy," writes Kathleen Riehle in her book, *What Smart People Do When Losing Their Jobs.* "If you know what to expect, you can be better prepared to deal with the impact on your life."

Unfortunately, there are no short cuts through this emotional roller coaster. After shock and anger come feelings of fear and denial. Feelings of fear are often tied to concerns about money. "If only" scenarios run rampant: "If only I had turned the report in earlier; if only I attended our company picnic," explains Beckhusen. "At this stage, you are holding yourself back from the emotional trauma of the loss to minimize its impact on you."

The lowest point of the emotional swings is depression. Signs of depression include avoiding people, erratic sleep, loss of appetite, feelings of helplessness, and hopeless thoughts. If you keep falling into this state, you may need to seek professional help.

Finally, acceptance of the situation leads to a release of anger, frustration, and fear. This is the turning point of the grief process. Beyond depression is the testing-out stage, where you start to explore different career options—attending job fairs, researching different jobs, and going on informational interviews.

The wild swings of emotion—from despair to elation and back into depression—make staying in bed in a dark room with sheets wrapped around your head seem like the best way to spend a Monday morning. Here are a few tips to ease you into the living room and out the front door to find a new job.

- Don't let your self-esteem take a beating because of a poorly handled firing or lay off. A company's rough treatment of you is due to its own incapacity to handle the situation and not an indication of your performance or you.

- If it's difficult to control your emotions immediately after being laid off, leave the office. Your former boss can be a great source of job prospects, a reference for a new job, and can provide resources for finding a new job—if you handle your firing or lay off well.

- As you negotiate your severance package, make sure you have adequately assessed your needs. Set up an appointment to discuss the issue one or two days after being laid off (don't wait too long, because your company may forget about you). After negotiating, have your employer put his commitments in writing.

- Seek out those who will support you. Going through this traumatizing experience alone only intensifies the emotional ups and downs. A support group helps you keep perspective. Job search groups provide a forum for support, acknowledgement, candor, and feedback. Other people or organizations who can provide support include the community center groups, friends, chamber of commerce job clubs, church groups, or a counselor, psychiatrist, or psychologist.

- Be aware that those that love you most—children, spouse, relatives— may also be fearful of your job loss, because their sense of security is jeopardized. They may not be your best supporters.

- One way you remain in an anxious or depressed state is to think obsessively about past events. Several psychologists suggested trying to picture yourself at your next job and how happy you will feel. When you are calm, your mind is clearer and you can make better decisions.

- To help your self-esteem, set goals where no rejection is involved. For example, go to the library and research a particular career field or company. So much about losing a job harms your self-esteem. You need to take care of yourself along the way to a new job.

- Wait until you've accepted your situation before you start making cold calls. During a state of depression is not the best time to put yourself in a high-risk situation. Nor is when you are in a fit of anger the best time to interview with a potential employer. One look at your rage and the employer will send you far, far away.

- Remind yourself that you may have lost your job, but you have not lost your skills or your experience. Some career counselors believe that this is a relatively good time to lose your job because you can always blame it on a bad economy.

- As in any stressful situation, eat well, exercise, and sleep to release stress. Exercise will give you energy and a sense of control, which you may lack right now. Eating well will also keep your energy high and help you avoid gaining weight.

- Ask yourself if you might have wanted this job change. "Often people subconsciously wanted to be let go," said several psychiatrists interviewed for this chapter. "At some level, they orchestrated the change." Once you've realized this, you can turn this loss into an opportunity for the job that you really wanted.

The Job Search

Now begins the process of finding a new job. For Jennifer Skinner, this has involved a complete reevaluation of her career, skills, values, and interests. Although she knows she could get a job, she wants to find the right job. She may take a part-time job to pay her bills as she searches for her new career. "But I feel that I owe it to myself to do what I really want to do," said Skinner.

Before you plunge into a different line of work, remember that to be eligible for unemployment benefits, you must be able and available for work. If the new job area is too different, you may be classified as unavailable for work. For example, if you've been in sales and suddenly decide you'd like to be an editor at a publishing company, the unemployment office will consider what skills you have to make you qualified for this new job. If you don't have the skills and you'll need schooling to change fields, the unemployment office will most likely deny you benefits. Check with the unemployment office to see if the retraining program you are interested in is approved. If so, you can continue to receive benefits even though you are not actively looking for a job.

Seated in a career development center's orientation room, Skinner joins thirty-five other people: some are recently laid off, some fired, and the majority are unhappy at their work. Over half admit that they do not know what they want to do next, but they are interested in trying to find out. A large chart in the front of the room highlights the steps to self-discovery.

"You're not alone in this process of self investigation," says the career counselor, reading people's minds as heads surreptitiously turn to glance around the room, wondering who else is entangled in a job search maze. "The process of finding the right job for you can become an obsession. The sight of a woman or man who is happy almost blows you over. You want to run up to her, grab her coat, look her in the eyes, and have her whisper her secret to you. You've got to know." Those in the room nod in agreement.

"Your instincts are right," explains the counselor. "Take this energy and start exploring what jobs are out there." Skinner starts to feel comfortable, almost at ease. The counselor explains that the concept of job satisfaction is relatively new, developed within the last fifteen years. "In the past, we did what we were apprenticed to do, because of our family, our place in society. For the first time, we can say that the sky's the limit."

The first step in the job search is self-assessment. In addition to many books on the subject, career development centers provide workshops to examine your values and past accomplishments and link them to marketable skills. Personality and aptitude tests create an inventory of accomplishments, skills, and interests. In the end, a comprehensive profile emerges. Career areas—communications, technology, computers—are identified and linked to job titles and names of companies.

Resource List for Self-Assessment
Before you go further with your job search, here is a brief summary of self assessment tools.

Books

What Color is your Parachute?, by Richard Nelson Bolles, published by Ten Speed Press, P.O. Box 7123, Berkeley, CA 94707.

Work With Passion: How to Do What You Love for a Living, by Nancy Anderson, copublication of Carroll & Graf Publishers, Inc. and Whatever Publishing, Inc., 260 Fifth Ave., New York, NY 10001.

Do What You Love, The Money Will Follow: Discovering Your Right Livelihood, by Marsha Sinetar, Paulist Press, 997 Macarthur Blvd., Mahwah, NJ 07430.

Take This Job and Love It, by Dennis T. Jaffe and Cynthia D. Scott, published by Fireside Books, Simon & Schuster Bldg., Rockefeller Center, 1230 Avenue of the Americas, New York, NY 10020.

Aptitude Testing/Skills Tests

Occupations Finder, by John L. Holland, Psychological Assessment Resources Inc., Box 998, Odessa, Fl 33556. This self-directed test helps you discover your interests and the occupations that are most compatible with those interests.

A Counselor's Guide to Career Assessment Instruments, by Jerome T. Kapes and Majorie Moran Mastie, published by the National Career Development Association, 5999 Stevenson Ave., Alexandria, VA 22304.

Myers-Briggs Test. Check the phone book for the local center in your area.

The Strong Interest Inventory, distributed by Consulting Psychologists Press, 577 College Avenue, Palo Alto, CA 94306. A 325-item questionnaire that inquires about your interests. The answers are analyzed by a computer and presented in a report.

Career Counselors

Look in the telephone directory under career counselors or outplacement companies.

Plan a Strategy
If you've identified several things that you'd like to do and are capable of doing, you'll have an easier time going through the job search process. Networking, resumes, cover letters, employment agencies, and informational interviews form the core of this step in the search.

With personal contacts accounting for some 60 to 70 percent of positions found, networking and informational interviewing are critical. "I made a list of everyone I knew," explained Cindy Abott, who found her job as a business manager at a newspaper through a friend. "Write down names of acquaintances, even if they do not work in your targeted career areas." Abott wrote down her doctor, minister, neighbors, old friends, former teachers, clients, casual acquaintances, bankers, fellow job-searchers—everyone she could think of went on the list.

Church meetings, community centers, professional luncheons, chamber of commerce job fairs, and former employers all provide possible job leads. "I avoided pressuring my friends by asking for advice rather than a job outright," said Abott. Abott phrased her approach something like this: "I'm making a career change right now, and I'd like fifteen minutes to ask your opinions and get some advice." According to Abott, "Everyone was so receptive. They wanted to give advice." Then, these people would give her more names to contact.

Executive search firms, hired by companies to locate executives, also provide leads to jobs. Employment agencies place employees in positions that pay up to $30-$40 thousand. These firms earn their fees only when an individual that they recommend is hired by a company. You pay nothing up front and can list your name with many agencies. Outplacement firms, hired by former employers, list jobs according to career areas. Temporary agencies are hired by companies to fill temporary openings, but placement may lead to a permanent job.

"Temporary jobs are also a great way to try out a job and see if you like it," said one president of a temporary agency firm. "Temp jobs can also rebuild self-esteem as you continue to search for your ideal job." As you read in chapter three on benefits, in most states, you can continue to receive unemployment benefits as long as your temporary work pay is less than the benefit amount.

It's been four weeks now since Jennifer drew the large reflection pool on her design for the senior citizen's park. Although bills now cover her front hall table and three different versions of her resume consume computer bytes on her Macintosh, she's discovered that she wants to work more closely to protect the environment. She talks excitedly about drought resistant plants and minimizing impacts on the land in her next job. She draws sketches of urban plazas with low trees and places to stroll. This is the longing that motivated her to become a landscape architect ten years ago. Now, giving her passion the room to breathe again, she trusts that it will take her to a different career path, maybe a land conservation organization, or an environmental group where her love for the land and her past experience—planting thousands of trees on her drafting paper—can grow.

Job Hunting Avenues

Here are the major ways to find out about job openings. Some career counselors advise you to try all of them and send out as many resumes as possible. According to one study, only one job offer is tendered and accepted for every 1,470 resumes that are sent out. So, if you're number 1,470, you get the job.

Others say to focus on those that have proven most effective in the past, such as finding job openings through friends. In job search books, you can find a more detailed explanation of how to use the following avenues to a new job.

- Networking with friends, relatives, trade organizations: This method has proven the most effective. If you're picking and choosing among different avenues, don't skip this one.

- School Placement Services: Check out the *Directory of Career Planning and Placement Offices*, published by the College Placement Council, Inc., 62 Highland Ave., Bethlehem, PA 18017. Also visit your local community college career placement center for job leads.

- Private Employment Agencies: There are roughly 8,000 agencies in the U.S., many specializing in executive, financial, legal, and data-processing areas. Check the telephone directory for your local agencies. Make sure you inquire who pays their fees—you or the employer.

- Job Fairs: Contact your local chamber of commerce or small business administration office for dates and times.

- Temp Jobs: Find this book in your library; *The Temporary Help Supply Service and the Temporary Labor Market*, by Donald Mayall and Kristin Nelson, published by Olympus Research Corp., 1670 E. 13th South, Salt Lake City, UT 84105.

- Newspaper Ads: Answering newspaper ads account for only 5 percent of the jobs found, according to career consultants.

- Executive Search Firms: These firms are recruiting companies retained by employers. To find local executive search firms and what areas they specialize in, locate these books in your library: *Directory of Executive Recruiters*, published by Consultant News, Templeton Rd., Fitzwilliam, NH 03447, which lists several hundred firms and industries served; and the *Directory of Personnel Consultants by Specialization*, published by the National Association of Personnel Consultants, Round House Square, 3133 Mt. Vernon Ave., Alexandria, VA 33205.

- United States Employment Services: Every states' office has access to the Interstate Job Bank listings, which tells you about opportunities in other states or cities. The typical number of listings is around 6,000. Look in the phone book under "Job Service," or "Employment Development Department," or the "State Unemployment Office."

- Registers: These are listings of job vacancies in particular industries—teachers, government jobs, nonprofit organizations and general business, outdoor jobs, overseas work, and criminal justice jobs. The registers also list both employers and people out of work. Try the *National Business Employment Weekly*, published by the Wall Street Journal, 420 Lexington Ave., New York, NY 10170, (212) 808-6792, a weekly compilation of career advancement positions. Or try the register for government jobs: *Federal Career Opportunities*, 370 Maple Ave., W., Box 1059, Vienna, VA 22180. These are just two examples of many kinds of registers available for specific job areas.

Resource List for Resume Writing and Interviewing

- *The Resume Solution: How to Write (and Use) A Resume that Gets Results*, by David Swanson, published by JIST Works, Inc., 720 North Park Avenue, Indianapolis, IN 46202-3421.

- *The Perfect Resume,* by Tom Jackson, published by Anchor Press/ Doubleday, Garden City NY 11530.

- *Knock 'Em Dead with Great Answers to Tough Interview Questions,* by Martin John Yate, published by Bob Adams, Inc., 260 Center St., Holbrook, MA 02343.

- *Q: How Do I Find the Right Job? A: Ask the Experts,* by David Bowman and Ronald Kweskin, published by John Wiley & Sons, Inc., 605 Third Avenue, New York, NY 10158.

Stress

Many people respond well to the stress in their lives. Their upbringing and different experiences create a high threshold for the amount of stress that they can manage. Although overloaded with responsibilities, these people view problems as challenges which they are capable of overcoming. Rather than ignoring difficult situations, these men and women acknowledge them and try to find solutions. If they don't have the solution, they get help in addressing the situation. Just hearing themselves talk about their how their self-esteem is suffering because they are out of work relieves stress. They also try and balance their work lives by including exercise, close friendships, and family. "There's a sense of control over their lives," said Dr. Beverly Potter, author of the book *Beating Job Burnout,* "a sense of well-being about themselves because they are creating their worlds."

Unemployment brings with it heightened levels of stress because of the uncertainty and lack of control over your life. What was once exciting is now a chore. You linger before getting out of bed. You see everything, including yourself, in a negative light. Under these conditions, it's nearly impossible to respond calmly when you receive a rejection letter or your first-grader dumps crayons on the swept kitchen floor.

If you don't slow down and take away some of the stress, your body may do it for you. You become more accident-prone. Tension shows up as frequent headaches, recurring colds, tight muscle, and changes in eating habits and weight.

When some people feel overwhelmed with stress, they respond in ways that only make matters worse: by ignoring the symptoms, finding ways to escape, or blaming others. Yet none of these approaches accounts for the drastic changes your body undergoes every time you face a stressful situation. Whether it's a job interview or a black bear attack, your body automatically mobilizes and prepares to physically act, whether this response is effective or not. This process, called the fight or flight phenomenon, uses up a tremendous amount of energy. Yet a finite amount exists, so you need time to replenish it by removing yourself from stress.

But if you are always in stressful situations, you eventually sap all your energy.

Fortunately, there are different methods that you can use to alleviate stress. We've talked about the first one—developing a job search plan. By using some kind of strategy, you gain a sense of control over your life. You are an active participant in your job search. The other methods are more personal. No one can follow all of these suggestions all of the time. But keeping them in mind may put you back in touch with who you want to be.

Tips for Dealing with Stress

- The first step is to develop an awareness of stress and the way your body reacts. Rather than always thinking something is wrong with you—you've always been and always will be an angry person—you can diagnose yourself more accurately.

- Since stress often shows up in physical ailments, listening to your body will tell you how much pressure you are under. Chronic tiredness may mean the load is too heavy or your days are not full enough. If your muscles are tense, your body may be craving activity. Write down how much stress you feel each day for three weeks. Give it a numerical rating. Then, describe any physical changes that occur. Notice the patterns emerging.

- With this greater understanding, you will see the sources of stress in your life more easily. Write down all the things you, your friends, and others complain about in a typical week. This list will sensitize you to the prevalence of stress in your life and help you to recognize the causes of pressure.

- Take a stress inventory. On a sheet of paper, list the major frustrations you feel in the week. Now circle items that are related to stress. Maybe some of these stressors can be eliminated—phone interruptions during dinner, parking problems, planning too much in one day.

- Take control of what you perceive as stressful. Develop a mental picture of a stressful event and, like a photograph, enlarge it. Keep enlarging it to the point where you'd move or take drastic action. Take a few minutes now and monitor your stress response. Maybe your stomach tightens or you breath rapidly. Notice that you are making this happen with a stressful image. You decide what pushes your buttons. Now reduce the picture. Test your feelings again. This exercise will increase your ability to create and control your perceptions.

- Set realistic goals and expectations for yourself and for others. "Give yourself win situations," said Dr. Beverly Potter. Make a list of what you'd like to accomplish during the day. For example, send out four resumes or call your former employer. "Work incrementally toward a goal, then reward yourself along the way." This is a way to develop personal power, giving you a sense of control over your life.

- Change gears and shift from your job search to something entirely different. Find something that contrasts with your typical day. If you've been alone all day, join a support group at night. Take a physical break—a walk or run—to divide up the day into job search time and personal time.

- Exercise at least three times a week. This is one of the best ways to fight sickness, depression, and fatigue. Try and eliminate excessive sugar, alcohol, caffeine, and nicotine from your diet.

- Pamper yourself. Break your routine—get a massage, take a warm bath, meditate, especially when you are aware of extra stress in your life. Learn relaxation techniques like meditation or yoga.

- Develop a support group of friends. As mentioned in the job search section, your friends are often your best source of job leads as well.

Financial Planning

For many people, the loss of income is the most terrifying part about being unemployed. If you managed to save a little from your paycheck each month, you may have bought yourself several months of time to look for a job. If you were living paycheck to paycheck, you need to scour your personal budget. And if you were deep in debt while you were employed, you need to gain control of your finances immediately.

Practically everyone owes money to someone for goods or services that they have already received. With the loss of income from your job, you need to consider how much money you owe, whom you owe it to, and where the money will come from to pay them back. Depending on how much debt you owe, getting out of debt will take anywhere from a couple of weeks to several years. If you know that you're in deep and don't want to read on, you can call a credit counselor right now. The most prominent service is the Consumer Credit Counseling Services (CCCS). This organization is funded through voluntary, tax-deductible contributions from major creditors, corporations, and employers. You receive free budget counseling and pay a minimal fee for debt management services.

How much do you owe? How much do you have? Start by pulling out all your personal finance records. Here is a list of some records that you will need to find:

1. Paycheck stubs;
2. Canceled checks for the last three months;
3. All your bills: utilities, phone, credit card bills, insurance bills. If the amounts have fluctuated a great deal, call your creditors and request copies of last year's bills;
4. Any contracts you signed to purchase goods;
5. Bank statements, loan books, any bank records.

Now, make a list of everyone you owe money to. Write down the creditor's name (the person whom you owe money to is a creditor), account number, address, and phone number. List any creditors to whom you have spoken to and the date. You will use this later to determine who to pay first.

What is your financial position?

Take that stack of papers and organize it into a worksheet of your financial position. Here is a sample.

SAMPLE BUDGET

Monthly Income $_____
Spouse's income   _____
Interest from Bank Accounts   _____
Other income   _____
        Total (1) $_____

Monthly Expenses:		**Annual Expenses:**	
Rent or Mortgage	$_____	Taxes	$_____
Food	_____	Insurance	_____
Utilities: gas, water,		Medical and dental bills	_____
sewage, phone,		School costs	_____
electricity, garbage	_____	Major purchases/repairs	_____
Savings and Investments	_____	Vacation	_____
Insurance	_____	Clothing	_____
Charitable contributions	_____	Interest expense	_____
Transportation	_____	Subscriptions, gifts	_____
Entertainment	_____	Other	_____
Other	_____	Total $_____	
Total (2) $_____		(÷ total by 12 to get monthly expenses)	
		Total (3) $_____	

Payments on current debts:

Personal loans—Name of lender	Monthly payment	Balance
_____	_____	_____
_____	_____	_____
_____	_____	_____
Charge accounts/installment payments	_____	

     Total (4) payments on current debts $_____

Add Total (2) Monthly expenses and $_____
Total (3) 1/12 Annual expenses and $_____
Total (4) Payments of current debts $_____
        Total (5) $_____

Subtract your total expenses from any monthly income:
(Total (1) $_____) Minus (Total (5) $_____) = Your monthly savings or debt

If you ended up in debt, you need to consider three approaches: meeting with a credit counselor, declaring bankruptcy, or managing your debt. If you are thinking of filing for bankruptcy, you need to speak with a lawyer. If you decide to develop a debt management plan, here are some things to consider.

Before you panic, take a look at your net worth. You may be able to sell off some of these items to get out of debt.

Net Worth: What you Own

Cash on hand/ Bank accounts (savings and checking)	$_____
Certificates of Deposit	$_____
Savings Bonds	$_____
Cash value of life insurance	$_____
Cash value of pension plan	$_____
Cash value of profit sharing plan	$_____
Severance	$_____
Market value of home	$_____
Market value of any real estate	$_____
Market value of business interests	$_____
Market value of securities	$_____
Market value of car, boat	$_____
Market value of household furnishings	$_____
Collections (stamp, art)	$_____
Other assets	$_____
Total	**$_____**

To make sure your asset prices are current, do the following: Call your real estate agent to find out the current market value of your house and any real estate you own. Also find out if housing prices have been rising or falling. You can check in the Kelley blue book for the price of your car. Figuring out your household belongings is difficult. For a conservative number, take 25 percent of the original price of the good and then take half that amount. Some of these things—boats, cars, things you haven't used around the house—can be sold, leased, or rented. Now, get a total. This is how much you've gotten in return for all that debt.

Before you read on, if you desperately need to solve an emergency situation because of the debt you owe, you first need to recognize that you have some power. Sears would rather not take back the used refrigerator in your kitchen or the couch in the living room. They would rather have your money. Set up an appointment to talk with a creditor counseling service or a lawyer. Starting now, everything you do should be in writing—conversations, dates, phone calls, people you talk to about resolving your debt situation. After meeting with either the counselor or an attorney or contacting an organization like Debtor's Anonymous, most likely you will have been told to make contact with your creditors—write them a letter explaining that you want to repay them and also give them a time frame of when they can expect to be paid. Mention that you've met with the counselor and are devising a debt management plan. The important thing is to make contact with the creditor to slow down their collection process.

With that letter out of the way, you need to develop a debt management program, whether you are under an emergency situation or you just want to get that stack of bills off your front desk. Discovering where your money is coming and going shows you where you can cut back. Look at every item in your budget and ask if each one is necessary. How many times a week do you pick up fast food or go out to dinner? Is public transportation an option instead of buying gas and paying for a parking spot? Take a look at your refrigerator. Have you overbought so that now food is wasting? Some of these things seem trivial, but the money adds up. Although credit counselors may not suggest that you cut up your credit cards, they do recommend paying for everything with cash or by check, not by credit card.

To establish a repayment plan, you need to consider your creditors. You should probably start by paying off the little guys—your relatives, small grocery on the corner, your doctor—because they are hurt most and, in some cases, charge the highest interest on late payments. This doesn't mean that they get paid off first, only that you make contact with them first and figure out a repayment plan. Then comes everyone else— car, furniture, Visa, any other credit cards, collection agency. By setting up priorities and meeting with your creditors, you will start to gain control over your finances. In both cases, the little and the big creditors, write a letter first so that everything is documented. In that letter, you should explain why you haven't been able to pay, suggest a reasonable and realistic amount that you can pay per month, and reassure them that you don't intend to increase your credit obligations at this time.

Financial Resources

- Debtor's Anonymous: Check your telephone directory for your local organization.

- Consumer Credit Counseling Services: Free budget counseling. Check your telephone directory for your local office.

- *You Can Go Bankrupt Without Going Broke*, by Lawrence R. Reich and James P. Duffy, published by Pharos Books, 200 Park Avenue, New York, NY 10166.

- *Getting Out From Under,* by Kenneth W. Bley, published by Consumer's Press, 1050 N. State Street, #200, Chicago, IL 60610.

- *Money Troubles: Legal Strategies to Cope with Your Debts,* by Robin Leonard, published by Nolo Press, 950 Parker Street, Berkeley, CA 94710.

- *Debtors' Rights: Self-Help Legal Guide*, by Gudrun M. Nickel, published by Sphinx Publishing, P.O. Box 25, Clearwater, FL 34617.

Other Social Services

Social Security Disability

If you suffer from a severe disability, you can collect social security disability checks if your former job was covered under the Social Security system. There is a list of impairments compiled by the Social Security Administration that are covered under this program. If your disability doesn't appear on the list, you must show that your condition is severe and prevents you from performing your former job or other comparable work.

Go to your local Social Security Administration office and submit a medical history and a statement from your doctor. Also submit information about your work history and education.

Workers' Compensation

If you were injured on the job, you and your family can receive compensation if your job was covered under this system. Check with your state department of labor. You will receive a fixed weekly amount, the size of which depends on your regular salary. Generally, you can recover the costs of hospitalization, medical care for the injury, and necessary rehabilitation.

If you aren't covered by a worker's compensation plan, you can sue your employer, but you must show that your injury resulted from your employer's carelessness.

Disability Benefits

Five states and Puerto Rico pay disability benefits. If you become ill or disabled while not at work, whether you are employed or unemployed at that time, you can collect disability benefits in California, New Jersey, Puerto Rico, Rhode Island, New York, and Hawaii. California also includes people infected with a communicable disease, acute alcoholics and drug addicts undergoing treatment.

Three states and one dependency—California, New Jersey, Rhode Island, and Puerto Rico—administer their disability programs through the office where you receive unemployment benefits. You can get information about disability benefits from the unemployment benefits office. In New York, contact the workmen's compensation board. And in Hawaii, contact the Temporary Disability Insurance Division of the Department of Labor and Industrial Relations.

Welfare

Welfare or general assistance is a state-mandated program that requires counties to provide support for their poor residents who have no other means to address their basic needs. It is primarily for single adults and childless couples. You must meet certain criteria such as a low income level, few assets, low rent payment and must not have quit a job without good cause.

AFDC is a nationwide program that provides poor families with monthly checks to help pay for basic needs such as rent, food and clothing. Families eligible for AFDC also receive health care and most get Food Stamps. You can apply for AFDC for you and your children if the children are "deprived:" a biological parent is deceased, continuously absent, ill, or unemployed.

Interesting Job Search Facts

- The typical job search lasts anywhere from eight to twenty-three weeks.

- Two-thirds of all job hunters spend five hours or less a week on their job hunt. Yet career counselors recommend spending thirty hours a week.

- The more ways you use to find a job, the greater chances of finding one. The average job hunter uses less than two ways.

- Job hunters interview with six employers a month. Career counselors recommend at least two a day—one in the morning and one in the afternoon—at a minimum.

- Two-thirds of new jobs are created in organizations with twenty or less employees.

Appendix

Sample Forms

SAMPLE

State of California
Employment Development Department

Notice of Determination/Ruling

Number 93 15 699

Date Mailed 03/27/93
Benefit Year Began 03/01/93

Jane Doe
1221 8TH AVE
Los Angeles   CA 96818

EDD FIELD OFFICE: 1680
AVALON SERVICE CENTER
161 WEST VENICE BLVD
LOS ANGELES CA
Telephone: (213) 744-2660

You are not eligible to receive benefits under California Unemployment Insurance Code Section 1256 beginning 03/01/92 and continuing until you return to work after the disqualifying act and earn $838 or more in bona fide employment, and reopen your claim.

You were discharged for repeated refusals to work during work hours. Therefore it must be held that you were discharged for actions which injured, or tended to injure your employer's interests. Section 1256 provides-an individual is disqualified if the department finds he voluntarily quit his most recent work without good cause or was discharged for misconduct from his recent work. Section 1268A provides-an individual is disqualified under section 1256 is not eligible for benefits until he has again worked in a bona fide employment and earned five times his weekly benefit amount.

If you have reason to believe that this decision is not correct, you may appeal it. You may request an appeal form from the office where you are now filing or you may write a letter of appeal to that office. The reasons why you do not agree with this decision must be written in your appeal.

While an appeal is pending you must continue to file a weekly claim in the field office for each week that you contend you are eligible. If the final decision holds you eligible, you can be paid only for those weeks for which you have filed a weekly claim and met all other eligibility requirements.

Any appeal from this notice must be filed on or before 04/16/93 to be timely.

APPEAL TO THE
CALIFORNIA UNEMPLOYMENT INSURANCE APPEALS BOARD

DECISION ISSUED BY:

In the matter of the Claim of:

_____OFFICE OF APPEALS

Case No._____XX5432_____which was

Judy Doe
_____
(Claimant)

mailed_____May 5_____, 19__93___.

_____
(Address)

_____
(Last Employer)

_____
(City)   (State)

_____
(Address)

_____
(Social Security Account No.)

_____
(City)   (State)

The appellant appeals and alleges that the decision of the Administrative Law Judge is in error on the following grounds:

STATEMENT OF FACTS:

I do not agree with the decision.

REASONS FOR DECISION:

(Use extra sheet, if necessary)

Note: In accordance with Section 1334 of the Unemployment Insurance Code, this appeal to the California Unemployment Insurance Appeals Board must be filed within twenty (20) calendar days after the DATE OF MAILING of the decision. ANY APPEAL FILED BEYOND THIS TWENTY-DAY PERIOD SHOULD CONTAIN AN EXPLANATION OF THE DELAY. (Enter explanation below if the appeal is filed more than twenty (20) calendar days beyond the mailing date of the decision.)

Date _____ , 19 ____ .

[Signed] _____

If completed
by an agent:

_____
(Duly authorized agent)

_____
(Address)

Mail 3 copies to: THE OFFICE OF APPEALS THAT ISSUED THE DECISION FROM WHICH YOU ARE APPEALING. THEIR ADDRESS APPEARS ON THE NOTICE YOU RECEIVED WITH YOUR COPY OF THE DECISION.

For Field Office use only. Filed at the _____ office of the Department,

No. _____ on _____ , 19 ____ .

_____
Department Representative

DE 1253 Rev. 17 (4-89)

CONTINUED CLAIM

EACH COLUMN IS FOR ONE WEEK ENDING AT MIDNIGHT OF THE DATE SHOWN.
ANSWER EACH QUESTION. For explanation of questions see section in Handbook entitled "Continued Claim Form." For prompt payment submit immediately after the week(s) has ended but not later than 14 days from the last week ending date shown. If extra space is needed, write on the back (Item D).

	1ST WEEK ENDS	2ND WEEK ENDS

1. **Did you work in that week?** If during or after either week you did any work in self-employment or for → another person, fill out Section A and/or B below.

2. **How much did you earn before deductions that week, whether you were paid or not?** If you → had no earnings that week, write "none". Tips, holiday pay, self-employment income are considered wages.

3. **Were you physically able to work full time each of the seven days that week?** If not, give → reason, dates, and time you were not able to work

4. **Was there any other reason you couldn't have worked full time each workday that week?** . → If yes, give reason, dates, and time you could not work

5. **Did you try to find work for yourself that week?** If not, please explain →

☐ ← IF MARKED "X", YOU MUST COMPLETE ITEM C, WORK-SEARCH RECORD, ON THE BACK OF THE FORM.

6. **Was any work offered you that week?** If yes, give starting date of job and name of employer, or → explain reason for refusal on the back of this form.

7. **Did any person in this office or anywhere else offer you a referral to a job that week?** → If yes, who offered the referral, on what date, and what was the result?

8. **Did you enroll in or attend any school or training that week?** . . . . → If yes, give starting date, days and hours of classes and your occupation on the back of this form.

9. **Did you have a change of address or phone number in that week?** . . . . →

If you moved, could you have worked if a job had been offered? ☐ Yes ☐ No   Date(s) of move?_____
NEW ADDRESS _____ NEW PHONE _____

10. **Are you receiving a pension other than Social Security?** . . . . →

If there has been a change in the amount of your pension, enter the new gross amount here $_____ and explain the reason for the change on the back of this form (item D).

(Right margin vertical text: F O L D / H E R E ↓)

A	DATES WORKED From / To	TOTAL HOURS WORKED	EMPLOYER - NAME AND ADDRESS	REASON NO LONGER WORKING
1ST WEEK				
2ND WEEK				

B   If you began or will begin work after weeks shown on this form enter beginning date_____ . Still working? ☐ yes ☐ no.
     If yes   ☐ Full Time   ☐ Part Time
     Employer's name_____

I have read, or had someone read to me, the questions and answers on this form. The answers are true and correct to the best of my knowledge. I understand that the law provides for a fine and/or imprisonment for making false statements or withholding facts to receive benefits.

DE 4581 Rev. 35 (11-89)

X _____
YOUR SIGNATURE   DATE

C. IF BOX UNDER QUESTION 5 ON THE REVERSE IS MARKED "X", COMPLETE THE TABLE BELOW. LIST THE EMPLOYERS THAT YOU CONTACTED IN SEARCH OF WORK DURING THE WEEK(S) BEING CLAIMED, TOGETHER WITH OTHER INFORMATION REQUIRED.

WORK-SEARCH RECORD (NOTE: ALL LISTED JOB CONTACTS MAY BE SUBJECT TO EMPLOYER VERIFICATION.)					RESULTS WRITE "YES" OR "NO" AS APPROPRIATE				
DATE YOU APPLIED	EMPLOYER	NAME OF PERSON CONTACTED	STREET ADDRESS, CITY, STATE	TYPE OF WORK APPLIED FOR	LEFT APPLI-CATION?	CALL BACK?	JOB OFFERED?	OTHER (EXPLAIN)

D. USE THIS SPACE FOR ADDITIONAL EXPLANATION

_____
_____
_____

☐ **CLAIMANT** — YOUR CLAIM IS BEING RETURNED TO YOU FOR CORRECTION AND/OR ADDITIONAL INFORMATION. Follow the instructions checked below, sign, date, and return this claim form as soon as possible, but no later than 14 days from this date: _____

DATE   EDD REPRESENTATIVE

☐ 1. Answer the items checked in red on the reverse side of this form.

☐ 2. This claim for benefits was submitted or postmarked before the last week ending date shown on this form. Benefits may not be claimed for a week until after that week has ended. Please check that all of your answers are correct for each week.

☐ 3. On the reverse of this form you have reported you did not work and had no earnings in answer to questions #1 and #2 for the week(s) ending _____ , but in Item A or B you show you started to work during the week ending _____ . Please correct your answers, or explain in detail in Item 7 below.

☐ 4. On the reverse of this form you have reported you did not work and had no earnings in answer to questions #1 and #2. Our records show the last day worked was _____ , which was during the week ending _____ . Please review your answers and correct if appropriate or explain in Item 7 below.

☐ 5. On the reverse of this form in question #1 you reported that you worked during the week ending _____ . However, in Item A or B you show that you did not start working until after this week was over. Please correct your answers, or explain in Item 7 below.

☐ 6. On the reverse of this form in question #1 you reported that you worked during the week(s) ending _____ . However, you did not show any earnings in #2. Please enter your earnings and complete Item A or B or correct your answer to #1.

☐ 7. Answer the following question(s), or use this space to answer other questions: _____
_____
_____
_____

X _____

State of California / Employment Development Department   YOUR SIGNATURE   DATE

UNEMPLOYMENT INSURANCE APPEAL BOARD

NOTICE OF HEARING

CASE NO: 197-0001   Admin. Law Judge: Judy Rudy

Claimant: Jeremiah Bullfrog   CL Rep: NONE
          1100 Broadway
          San Francisco, CA

          SSA No: 66-48-585

Employer: ER Rep: NONE


```
-------------------------------------------------------------------
*                                                                 *
*    Date & Time: Tuesday, June 5, 1993 at 11:00 A.M.             *
*                                                                 *
*    Place: Franklin Street        San Francisco                 *
*                                                                 *
*    Note: Report to Appeals Waiting Section                      *
*                                                                 *
-------------------------------------------------------------------
```

IMPORTANT: Arrive ten minutes early: Be prompt: The time will be
necessary for you to examine dept. claim and interview records.
Bring to the hearing any witnesses, medical statements, employment
records, and other evidence. Failure by appellant to attend may
result in appeal dismissal.

Issues are: (Section references are in the Un. Ins. Code unless
otherwise stated.)

DETER
```
    ***************************************************
    *                                                 *
    *    To: Claimant  Employer                       *
    *    Please bring your copy of the determination  *
    *    to the hearing for use of the administrative *
    *    law judge.                                    *
    *                                                 *
    ***************************************************
```

Direct Inquiries to:

San Francisco Office of Appeals   Date Mailed: 5/14/93
Franklin Street, 4th Floor
San Francisco, CA

In the Matter of:

_____

_____Judy Doe_____

_____

_____

)
)
)   **DECLARATION FOR SUBPENA**
)   **DUCES TECUM OR FOR NOTICE TO**
)   **ATTEND HEARING AND/OR TO BRING**
)   **CERTAIN DOCUMENTS AND RECORDS**
)
)   _____XX37564_____ Appeals Case No.

_____ declares: That he is

_____ in the above-entitled matter;

that said matter has been duly set for hearing before an Administrative Law Judge of the California

Unemployment Insurance Appeals Board, on

_____July 8_____ at _____10:00 AM_____
            (Date)   (Hour)

☐ AT THE LOCAL OFFICE OF THE EMPLOYMENT DEVELOPMENT DEPARTMENT

☐ AT THE OFFICE OF APPEALS OF THE UNEMPLOYMENT INSURANCE APPEALS BOARD

☐ AT THE FIELD OFFICE HEARING ROOM OF THE UNEMPLOYMENT INSURANCE APPEALS BOARD

_____
            (Street Address)   (City)

That declarant is informed and believes and upon such information and belief alleges that

_____Frank Smith_____

_____
                        (Name of person who has records, etc.)

has in his possession or under his control the following documents:

(Name and Address and describe clearly the things to be produced.)

_____1234 Harbor Drive; Mr. Smith has all Ms. Doe's past work performance evaluations._____

_____

_____

Declarant believes and so states that the above documents are material to the proper presentation of his case

by reason of the following facts:

(State the materiality to the issues involved.)

_____Ms. Doe is charged with misconduct; Mr. Smith alleges that Ms. Doe consistently_____

_____broke valuable goods. But these records show that she always received excellent_____

_____reviews of her work._____

WHEREFORE declarant requests the issuance of a Subpena Duces Tecum or a Notice to Attend Hearing
and/or to Bring Certain Documents and Records.

*I DECLARE UNDER PENALTY OF PERJURY UNDER THE LAWS OF THE STATE OF CALIFORNIA THAT THE
FOREGOING IS TRUE AND CORRECT.*

_____   _____
            (Date)   (Sign here)

ISSUANCE OF: ____ Subpena Duces Tecum
             ____ Notice to Attend Hearing and/or to Bring Certain Documents and Records

              ____ APPROVED   ____ DISAPPROVED

                                    _____
                                    Administrative Law Judge   Date

Index

ALLWORTH PRESS BOOKS

Allworth Press publishes quality books to help individuals and small businesses. Titles include:

Legal-Wise: Self-Help Legal Forms for Everyone
by Carl Battle (208 pages, 8½" X 11", $16.95)

Senior Counsel: Legal and Financial Strategies for Age 50 and Beyond
by Carl W. Battle (256 pages, 6¾" X 10", $16.95)

Business and Legal Forms for Authors and Self-Publishers
by Tad Crawford (176 pages, 8⅞" X 11", $15.95)

Business and Legal Forms for Fine Artists
by Tad Crawford (128 pages, 8⅞" X 11", $12.95)

Business and Legal Forms for Graphic Designers
by Tad Crawford and Eva Doman Bruck (208 pages, 8½" X 11", $19.95)

Business and Legal Forms for Illustrators
by Tad Crawford (160 pages, 8⅞" X 11", $15.95)

Business and Legal Forms for Photographers
by Tad Crawford (192 pages, 8½" X 11", $18.95)

Legal Guide for the Visual Artist
by Tad Crawford (224 pages, 7" X 12", $18.95)

Careers By Design
by Roz Goldfarb (224 pages, 6¾" X 10", $16.95)

How to Sell Your Photographs and Illustrations
by Elliott and Barbara Gordon (128 pages, 8" X 10", $16.95)

The Business of Being an Artist
by Dan Grant (224 pages, 6" X 9", $16.95)

On Becoming an Artist
by Dan Grant (192 pages, 6" X 9", $12.95)

The Family Legal Companion
by Thomas Hauser (256 pages, 6" X 9", $16.95)

How to Shoot Stock Photos that Sell
by Michal Heron (192 pages, 8" X 10", $16.95)

ALLWORTH PRESS BOOKS

The Photographer's Organizer
by Michal Heron (192 pages, 28" X 10", $16.95)

Stock Photo Forms
by Michal Heron (32 pages, 8½" X 11", $8.95)

Accepted: Your Guide to Finding the Right College —and How to Pay for It
by Stuart Kahan (128 pages, 6¾" X 10", $10.95)

The Photographer's Assistant
by John Kieffer (208 pages, 6¾" X 10", $16.95)

Licensing Art & Design
by Caryn R. Leland (272 pages, 6" X 9", $18 .95)

Travel Photography: A Complete Guide to How to Shoot and Sell
by Susan McCartney (384 pages, 6¾" X 10", $22.95)

The Graphic Designer's Basic Guide to the MacIntosh
by Michael Meyerowitz and Sam Sanchez (144 pages, 8" X 10", $19.95)

Hers: The Wise Woman's Guide to Starting a Business on $2,000 or Less
by Carol Milano (208 pages, 6" X 9", $12.95)

The Artist's Complete Health and Safety Guide
by Monona Rossol (328 pages, 6" X 9", $16.95)

Stage Fright
by Monona Rossol (144 pages, 6" X 9", $12.95)

Electronic Design and Publishing: Business Practices
by Liane Sebastian (112 pages, 6¾" X 10", $19.95)

Overexposure: Health Hazards in Photography
by Susan Shaw and Monona Rossol (320 pages, 6¾" X 10", $18.95)

Caring for Your Art
by Jill Snyder (176 pages, 6" X 9", $14.95)

Make It Legal
by Lee Wilson (272 pages, 6" X 9", $18 .95)

Please write to request our free catalog.
If you wish to order a book, send your check or money order to:
Allworth Press, 10 East 23rd Street, Suite 400, New York, New York 10010
To pay for shipping and handling, include $3 for the first book ordered and $1 for each additional
book ($7 plus $1 if the order is from Canada). New York State residents must add sales tax.